Incredible but True

Publishers
Pustak Mahal®

Administrative office and sale centre
J-3/16 , Daryaganj, New Delhi-110002
☎ 23276539, 23272783, 23272784 • *Fax:* 011-23260518
E-mail: info@pustakmahal.com • *Website:* www.pustakmahal.com

Branches
Bengaluru: ☎ 080-22234025 • *Telefax:* 080-22240209
E-mail: pustak@airtelmail.in • pustak@sancharnet.in
Mumbai: ☎ 022-22010941, 022-22053387
E-mail: rapidex@bom5.vsnl.net.in
Patna: ☎ 0612-3294193 • *Telefax:* 0612-2302719
E-mail: rapidexptn@rediffmail.com

Other Sale Counters in Delhi
- 10-B, Netaji Subhash Marg, Daryaganj, New Delhi-110002
- 6686, Khari Baoli, Delhi-110006

ISBN 978-81-223-0350-6

Edition: 2012

Printed at : Super Fine Book Printing & Binding Works (U.P.)

Incredible but True

Harish Yadav
(*Translated by:* **Ms Seema Gupta**)

PUSTAK MAHAL®

CONTENTS

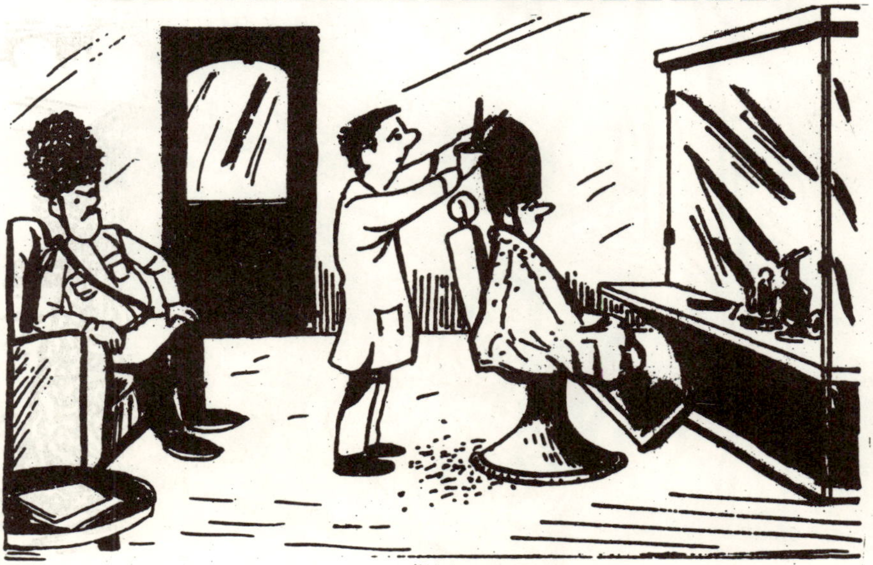

It's a baby

The three girls of Henriksen family in Norway celebrate their birthday on the same date. As it is, it's bad enough that they have to share their birthday cake; on top of it, they have to wait for four years before they can light the candles. On every 29 February, Heidi (born : 1960), Olav (born : 1964) and Lief Martin (born : 1968) can be seen pondering: How many candles this year? (*Guinness Book*)

It is like a family tradition; which started with Williams. Williams was born in Wilmington, North Carolina, USA, on 4 July, 1876, exactly 100 years after America got independence. His son Williams II was also born on 4 July. This was followed by his grandson, William III who too was born on 4 July. The latest in the line is his great grandson Ralph Bertram who was born on 4 July, 1982. True Americans! (*Guinness Book*)

The great grandmother Lorreta Willet was born on 29 May, 1897. For the next 66 years, she enjoyed her birthdays solely with all the glory bestowed upon her. 29 May 1963 brought in Le N Jinani, her first great grand-daughter and the first one in the family to share her birthday. Then came Christie Lin Jinani on 29 May, 1965; her second great granddaughter in the queue. The third great granddaughter Shenon Gerald too was born on 29 May, 1974. The birthdays may have been shared, it is the Great Grandma Lorreta Willet who takes the cake. (*Ripley*)

Ever heard of heredity — the characters which pass on from one generation to another through genes. But what if these characters are not genetic, but acquired. Louis Henri De Bourbon of France lost his left eye on a hunting mission in the year 1700. Later on, he became father of five sons. All the five sons were blind with their left eye, by birth. (*Ripley*)

Like father, like son. A very old saying but how it is true? It was proved in 1970 at Orphenbuck in West Germany. A woman Graty Berdum gave birth to twins. When she was shown both her sons, she fainted. The reason being that one baby was white with blue eyes and blonde hair whereas the other one was black with brown eyes and black hair. It was later revealed that Graty had physical contact with a German trader and a black American soldier on the same day. (*Book of List*)

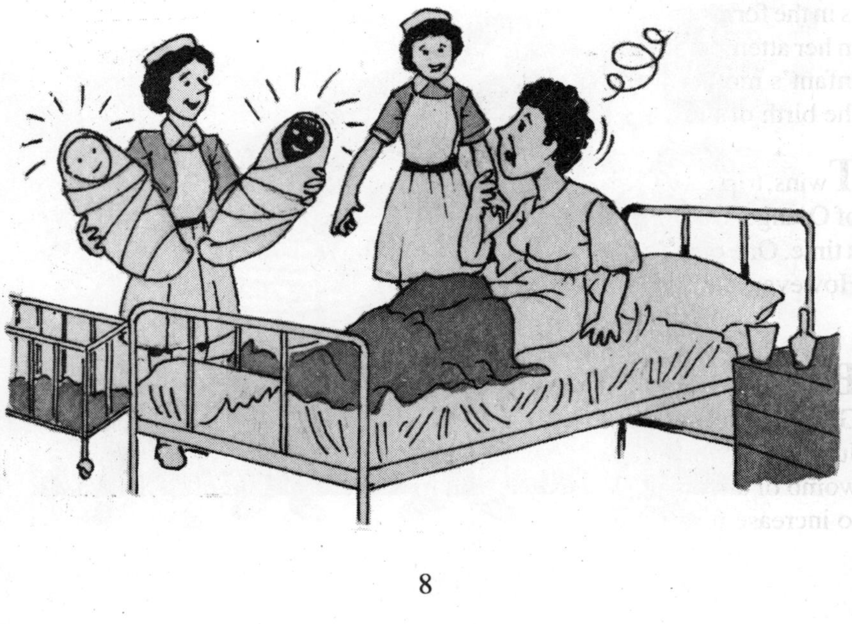

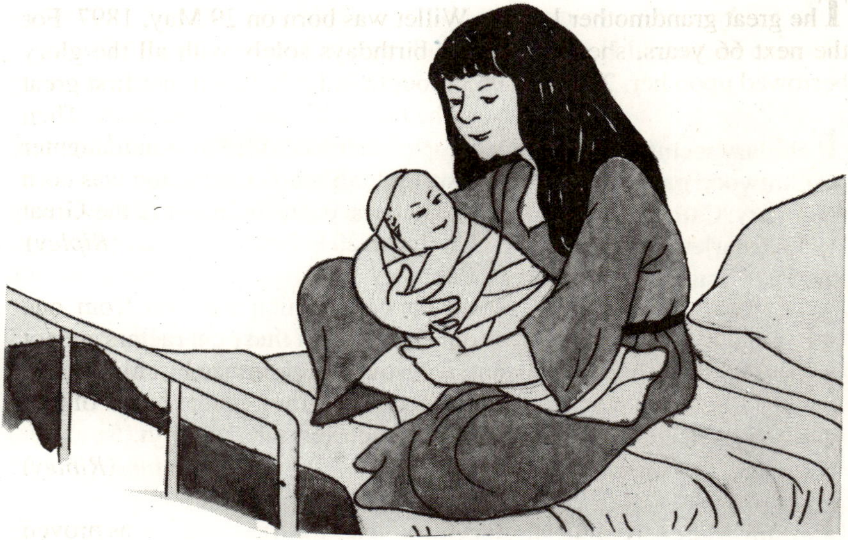

The world record for giving birth to the largest number of kids goes to Feodor Vassilyev's first wife. The woman gave birth to 69 kids during her lifetime (1725-1765). Out of these, 67 survived. Among her children were 16 twins, 7 triplets and 4 quadruplets. (*Guinness Book*)

Posthumous awards are tragic. But what would anyone do if this award is in the form of a baby. In Mangolia, Dr (Ms) Robert Drek was successful in her attempt to save a six-pound healthy baby on 15 October, 1966. The infant's mother Fennela Anderson breathed her last, 80 minutes before the birth of the baby. (*Guinness Book*)

Twins, triplets, even quadruplets have been superseded by Patti Jorgenson of Orange, California on 21 May, 1985. She gave birth to seven babies at a time. One of them was stillborn. Three of them died within a few weeks. However, the remaining three survived and led a normal life. (*Guinness Book*)

Beware! Those who have been taking medication for fertility. Dr Gennaro Montanino of Rome came across something most unusual on 22 July, 1971 when he had to clear a herd of 10 girls and 5 boys from the womb of a woman. The lady is said to have been taking some medicine to increase fertility. (*Guinness Book*)

On 5 July, 1983, a woman gave birth to a baby of 3 pound 11 ounces at Roanko Memorial Hospital. She had been in coma for last 84 days.

(*Guinness Book*)

February seems to be a month of repeated birthdays. Ralph and Caroline of Cintwood gave birth to five offsprings, all born on the same date — 20 February. Catherine was born on 20 February 1952, Carol on 20 February 1953, Charles on 20 February, Claudia on 20 February 1961 and fifth and the last Cicilia was born on 20 February 1966. (*Guinness Book*)

He who loves thy shall save thou! This was proved on 8 February, 1983 at San Diago, California when Arnehiston Hoodgins, an infant weighing merely 17 ounces was born eighteen weeks prior to the expected date of delivery. At the time of his birth, his mother was only 147 days (5 months) pregnant. The premature baby survived. (*Guinness Book*)

Emilio Marcos Palma of Argentina was the first one to be born at Antarctica. She was born on 7 January, 1978 at Sargento Cabral Base. The severe cold and icy winds marked her birth as a kind of its own. Her mother was sent to Antarctica by Argentinian government.

(*Guinness Book*)

In an amazing incident of multiple childbirth, Mrs Geraldine Broadrick of Australia gave birth to 9 children on 13 June 1971 at Royal Hospital, Sydney. There were 5 sons and 4 daughters. Out of the 5 boys, 2 were still born.

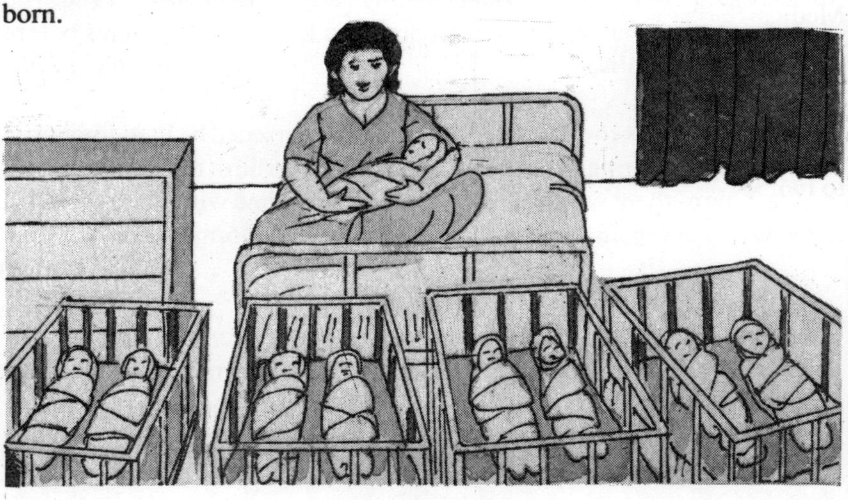

Sabrina Lien Henrick of Houston, Texas was born on 26 November, 1978. It was an important day in the family as her great grandmother, grandmother, uncle, aunt and nephew were all born on the same date.

(*Book of List*)

We have all heard of child brides, but ever heard of child mother? A 10-year-old girl gave birth to a baby boy of 5 pound 10 ounces in Alexandria on 29 July 1969. (*Book of List*)

Quite contrary to this happened in Johannesburg, South Africa where 58-year-old Davvy Du Placis delivered a 5-pound baby girl on 16 July 1969. At that time, Davvy was already a mother of 8 children and a grandmother of 12 kids. (*Book of List*)

When East and West Germany were getting reunited after 45 years of separation and the Berlin Wall was being demolished, Jacob Schreimer became the first citizen of united Germany. Ina Schreimer gave birth to this baby boy at midnight on 3 October 1990. (*Times of India*)

Future is so unpredictable. Who would have imagined that Ron Thompson of Austin, Texas, who was a grandfather of 5 children at lunchtime would become a proud grandpa of 9 grandchildren overnight. On 1 January, 1990, his three daughters Mrs Tallson John and Carol were blessed with four sons. On 1st afternoon, Mrs Tallson reached Seton Medical Centre accompanied by her sister John. She was in labour for five hours. She gave birth to a baby boy. Seven hours later, John also went into labour. She took her third sister Carol and went back to the hospital. At midnight, John too became mother of a baby boy. By now Carol, who too was pregnant, went into labour. Next morning at 3 O'clock she gave birth to twins.

(*The Hindu*)

Double trouble

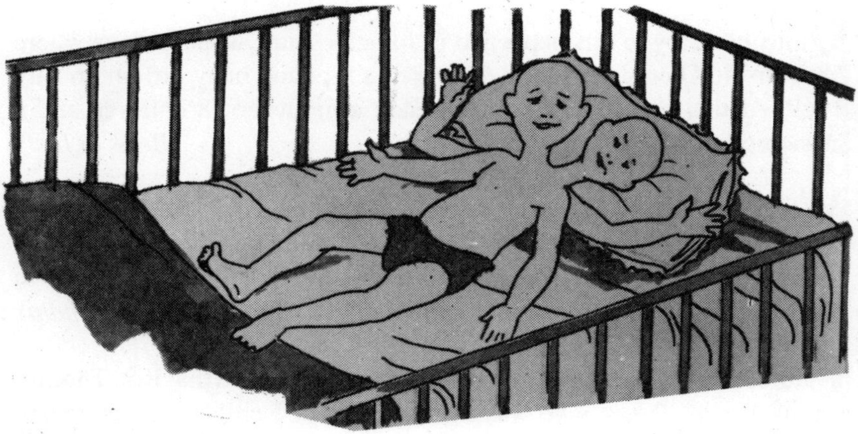

The rare Dicephales tetrabrachius dipus Siamese twins can be identified by their characteristic 2 heads, 4 arms and 2 legs. There are only three such twins in the world. (*Guinness Book*)

A true example of nature's forced togetherness are Chang and Eng Bunker. They were two siamese brothers who were joined by the skin of their chest. They were born in Thailand on 11 May, 1811. They led a normal life. They married two different girls and had 10 and 12 children respectively. They both died on 17 January, 1974 at the age of 62. (*Guinness Book*)

The lighter you are, the longer you live. A pair of twins weighs only 991 g at the time of their birth when even a single healthy child weighs four times more. Mary and Margaret of England weighed only 453 g and 538 g respectively at the time of birth. The girls survived merrily only to be declared as the lightest weight twins in the world. (*Guinness Book*)

The story of Scottish brothers is far more tragic. These two Siamese twins were born way back in 1490 in Scotland during the reign of King James IV. When one of the twins died in 1518, his counterpart had no choice but to carry the dead body of his brother as it was joined with his own body. For the next five days, he went through hell. He cried for help; he went to the doctors; he prayed to God; but all in vain. His suffering ended on the sixth day. He too died. (*Guinness Book*)

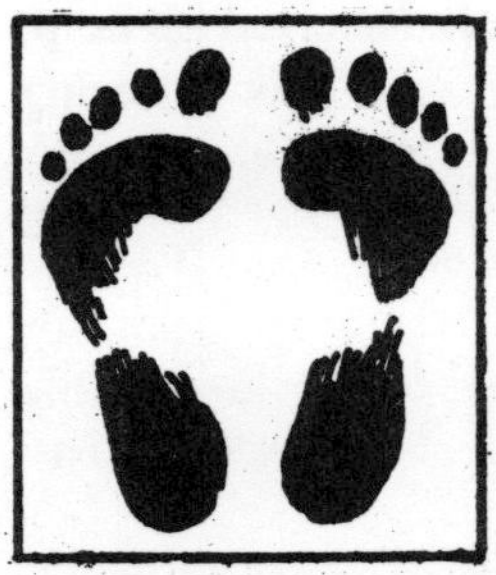

The ultimate

Even a good horse stumbles at times. The famous philosopher Francis Bacon (1561-1626) pondered one day, as to how the smell of a dead animal could be stopped by using ice. Francis bought a hen, killed it and stuffed it with ice. Immediately Francis started shivering and he died due to the exposure to severe cold. (*Book of List*)

A bridle for the tongue is a necessary piece of furniture. True! But one should be careful about its use. Allan Pinkerton (1819-1884) was the owner of an American Detective Agency. One fine day, he went to the loo. During the process, while putting some pressure, his tongue got caught between his teeth and was badly cut. It became septic and later gangrene. Finally it cost him his own life. (*Book of List*)

Arnold Bennett (1867-1931), a British author, was attending a meeting at Paris. Just to demonstrate that the water in Paris is clean and pure, he drank a glass of water in front of the audience. The water turned out to be contaminated. Arnold fell ill with typhoid and died. (*Book of List*)

A Turk wrestler Yusuf Ismail came to America in 1898. He defeated the American Wrestling Champion Ivan Lewis. Whatever money he earned from this wrestling match, Yusuf spent in gold coins. He hid the coins into his waistbelt. On the way back, his ship 'Le Bargon' collided with another English ship 'Nawa

Scottia'. When the ship started to sink, Yusuf's friends advised him to throw the heavy coins into the water so that he could swim freely to the shore. But he did not listen to them and jumped into the sea with the coins still intact in his waistbelt. The weight of the coins made it difficult for him to swim even for a mile. Though a good swimmer, he succumbed to his greed. All covet, all lost. (*Book of List*)

A thing of glory may sometimes prove to be the reason for one's end. Hans Steininger of Austria was famous for his beard which was the longest in the world. In September 1567, while climbing the stairs of Brunn's council chamber, he got entangled in his own beard. Hans lost his balance and fell down the stairs. He died on the spot. (*Book of List*)

Cleanliness is Godliness. But Pat Burke hated baths; so much so that he had not taken a bath for the past 20 years. On 23 August, 1903, he bathed for the first time in 20 years. However, it seems his body did not like this intrusion on its privacy. The very next day, Pat died in a hospital. (*Book of List*)

A Mexican General Rodulfo Fierro (1880-1917) was heading towards Sonara. On the way, he took a wrong turn and found his horse stranded in the marsh. General Rodalf was carrying huge quantity of gold with him. The heavy weight on the back of the horse pushed him deep inside the marsh. Within minutes, the General, the horse and the gold were buried deep down in the marsh. (*Book of List*)

The Italian poet Sabrino Farreiri was passing his time in a mental hospital when he got the unexpected news of his appointment at Bollona University as the professor of literature. The poet died out of sheer excitement. (*Book of List*)

It is a widely known fact that a small ant can kill a huge elephant but not many people know how a small fly killed the Pope Adrian IV. In 1159, the Pope was giving a speech. During the speech when he opened his mouth to drink some water, a fly came and stuck to the Pope's pallet. Even the best surgeons could do nothing. All efforts failed in removing the fly from Pope's throat. The fly proved to be the messenger of death. Never ignore it if you come across a fly in your cup of coffee. (*Book of List*)

Mark Twain was born in 1835. It was the same year when Halley's comet was seen. Twain had this superstition, that when this comet will return towards earth, he will die. And it happened. In 1910, this comet was seen once again. The same year, on 21 April, Mark Twain breathed his last. (*Book of List*)

Many may boast about the modern hi-tech machines. The machines will always remain mindless instruments. Japan experienced it not so long ago. Kenji Urada worked in a factory at Kawasaki Heavy Industries. On 4 July, 1981, he was killed by a robot just because Kenzie did not see the robot coming. Since he could not step aside in time, the robot, on finding something on its way, killed him. This was the first incident in which a robot killed a human being. (*Book of List*)

Number thirteen is supposed to be an unlucky number. But, for Austrian Musician Arnold Schonberg (1874-1951) this number proved to be both lucky as well as unlucky. Lucky in the sense that he was born on 13 September. Arnold had a strong belief that his death will also be connected with this number. His belief was confirmed when he died on 13 July, 1951 at the age of 76 (add: 13) at 11:47 (13 minutes before midnight). (*Book of List*)

Roy C. Sullivan was an amazing man. He was hit by the lightning not once or twice but seven times. Miraculously he survived each time. Later on, he committed suicide after a failed love attempt. (*Guinness Book*)

Excess of everything is bad. Tina Christopherson of Florida was 29-year-old when she started suspecting that she is suffering from abdominal cancer. She almost gave up food and started living on plain water. Whenever she was hungry she would drink water so much so that she drank 4 gallons of water in a day. On 17 February, 1977, she died of water intoxication. (*Book of List*)

Bobby Leach was a brave man. In 1911, he locked himself in a barrel and jumped into the Niagra Falls. Later, he repeated the same act with the help of a parachute, successfully. As the luck would have it, 15 years later, in April 1926, the same Bobby Leek slipped on an orange peel while on his way to Christ Church, New Zealand. His leg was amputated. After some time, Bobby died. (*Book of List*)

Shah Faizal of Saudi Arab was busy discussing some matters regarding oil supplies with his ministers when his nephew Prince Faizal Ibn Mussad Abdul Aziz entered the conference room. His arrival without prior information was most unexpected. The Shah assumed that Abdul might have come there for his blessings on that auspicious day of Saint Mohammad's birthday. In anticipation of the traditional kiss the Shah bowed his head. But the cruel nephew, instead of planting a kiss, shot the Shah on head and killed him. (*Book of List*)

In fifth century the Greek painter Zeuxis made a painting of an old witch. He found it so amusing that he could not stop laughing. It was like he had inhaled the laughing gas. He laughed so much that finally he died. If only he had known that it was not the old witch he was painting but the messenger of death, he would not have touched the canvas forever.

(*Book of List*)

'Dead Man's Hand'. James Butler Hickok was an expert in the cars' game. He was famous as 'Wild Bill'. James always played with his back towards the wall. Once he was playing 'Poker' in the club. That night just to tease his friend, James sat with his back towards the door. And someone killed him. Butler's last hand was three Aces and a pair of black eights. Since then this pair has been known as the 'Dead Man's Hand'.

(*Book of List*)

Calcus became famous for his genius when he conceived the idea of a wooden horse during the Battle of Troy. One day he was planting some grape vine in his garden. His friend who was passing by said that Calcus will not be able to taste the wine from these grapes. During the course of time, the wine was ready. Calcus, who had not forgotten his friend's words, invited him over for drinks. While holding the glass of wine in his hand, Calcus mocked at his friend's foolish comment. But the friend remained unperturbed. He repeated the same words. It amused Calcus so much that he started laughing. In a fit of laughter he choked and died. The full glass of wine was still in his hand.

(*Book of List*)

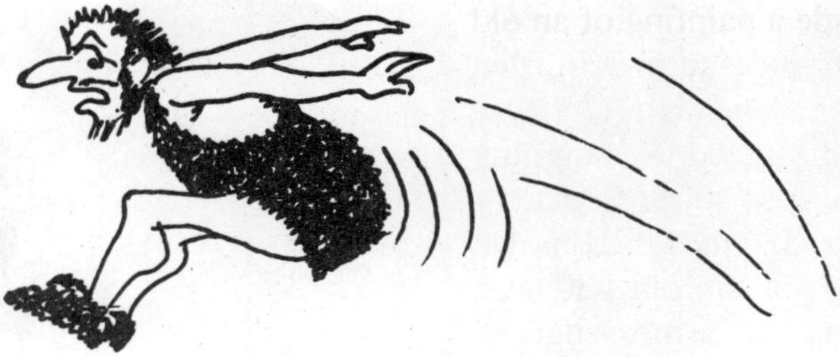

No vice like avarice. Mary Countess Arco of Austria found a box of gold coins in her garden. The coins were worth 50,000 dollars. She took them home but refused to spend a single penny out of her treasure. She was so possessive about it that wherever she went, she took the coins with her. While travelling, she would hide this box in a secret corner of her carriage. On 23 June 1948, a jolt in the carriage brought the hidden box out of its place and it fell on Mary's head who was sitting right under it. Mary died then and there.

(*Ripley*)

People drink wine, bathe in wine, many even swim in wine. But Richard III drowned his brother Duke George of Clarence in Wine.

(*Book of List*)

Francesco Del Bark invented a machine which could throw weights up to 1500 pound, far away, as a missile. In 1346, in an attack on Delmeta, Francesco was throwing stones with the help of his machine. During the process, he got entangled with the machine and instead of the stone, Francesco himself got thrown as a missile. He landed in a city through which his wife was passing. He fell on his wife. They both died.

(*Ripley*)

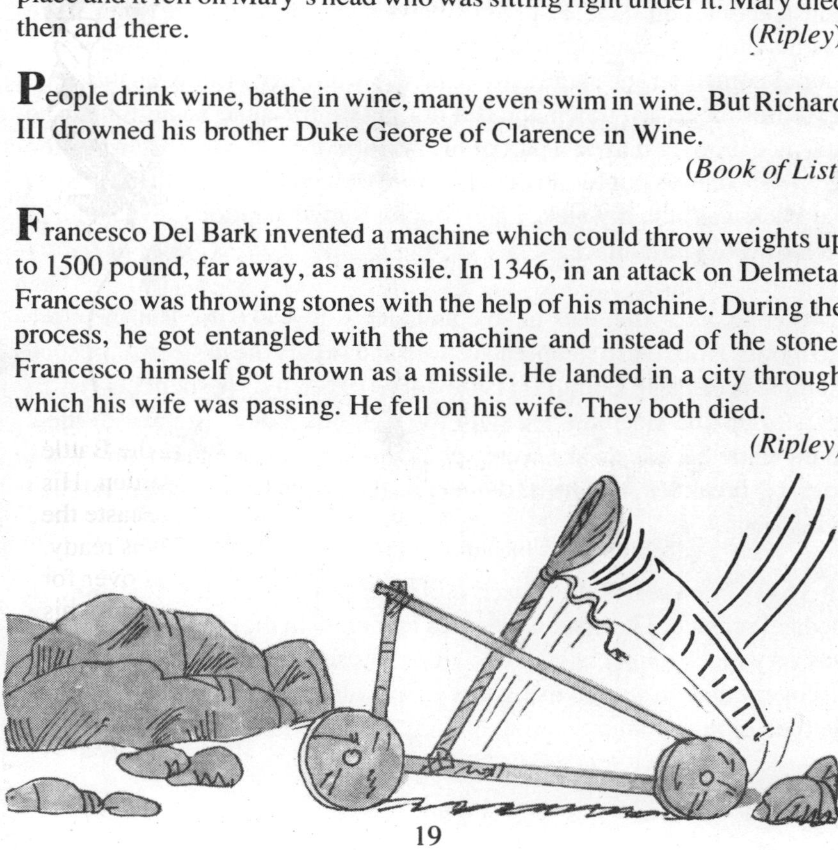

Could it be the case of one's loss and another's gain? In a report from Gabri village of Durg District, two boys were playing in a field when the lightning struck them. One of them died on the spot whereas the other who was dumb by birth got his speech back. (*Times of India*)

Al Shahrani was working in a factory when he fell down and went into a coma. His family members took him to be dead and buried him. About 27 hours later when he recovered consciousness, he started calling out from his grave. Some passers-by took him out. When he reached home, his mother and sister thought him to be a ghost and lost their mental balance. After a few days, Al was back to the same graveyard — burying his sister and mother. (*Times of India*)

According to Press Trust of India (PTI), a play was being staged in Dumaria Village. In this play *Khoon Ka Badla*, a scene required one actor to shoot at the other with a gun. The scene turned into reality when the other actor fell on the ground bleeding profusely. It was discovered later that the gun had real cartridge. The poor innocent victim died on the spot. (*Times of India*)

How the words can be misinterpreted at times? In 1799, Napoleon was working as a General in Middle East. One day he ordered his subordinates to free 1200 Turk prisoners. Just as he was giving the order, he started coughing. Cursing it he said 'Ma Sakri Taks' (This horrible cough) which was understood by his subordinates as 'Massacre Taous' (Kill them all). Poor 1200 prisoners became victims of a game of words. (*Ripley*)

A tombstone at England's Whiteby Churchyard reads as, "Francis Huntdraws and his wife Mary are buried here. They both were born on 19 September 1600 and got married on 19 September. They have 12 offsprings. Now at the age of 80 they both died on 19 September."

(*Ripley*)

In a motor workshop at Jakarta, two mechanics were working. One of them noticed that the other's pant is torn from the back. Just to play a harmless prank, he put the nozzle of the air compressor through the pant's hole. Unfortunately, the nozzle got stuck in the anus. Within seconds his body bloated with air and he died. (*Times of India*)

Can the books kill anyone! They did — in Paris. Three labourers were putting the books in a godown at Paris when the books from the upper shelf fell on them. All three of them died under the weight of the books.

(*Times of India*)

Moore Pultzer was 65 when he suffered a paralytic stroke in 1983. He was treated in a hospital where he was fed through tubes. Pultzer hated this life. He appealed to the court that he should be given permission to die as he did not want to carry on like this. The New Jersy court gave him the permission. Tube feeding was withdrawn. Soon after Pultzer died.

(*Times of India*)

■■

Diseases

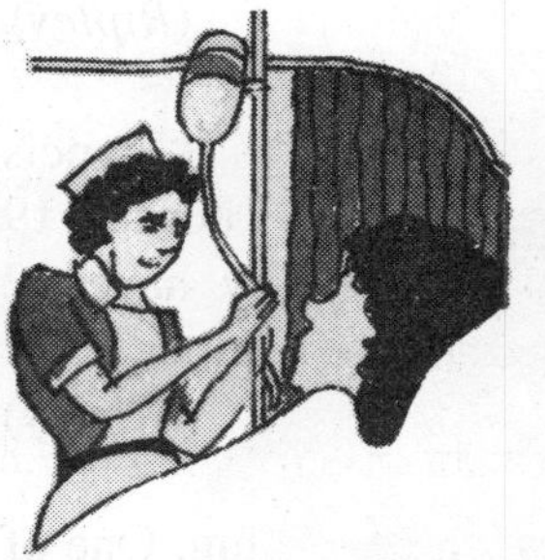

Progeria is a disease in which the patient starts ageing prematurely. His growth stops and with each passing year he shows the signs of ageing of ten years. This is a rare disease and the chances to acquire it are one in a million. Till date, only 85 such cases are known. One such victim was Francie Geringer of Africa. This 16-year-old young boy remained dwarf as his growth stopped. All his hair fell and his face was distorted. At the tender age of 16, he started looking like an old man of 160 years. His heart was in a bad condition and he had suffered many heart attacks. Seeing his deteriorating condition and considering the rarity of his disease the African government announced a special pension for Francie. But he could not enjoy it for long and died. (*Times of India*)

Sweating is a natural phenomenon. But what if someone can sweat at the drop of a hat! Parnella could do exactly this. He could bring out the sweat anywhere, anytime and in as much quantity as he desired.

(*Times of India*)

An actor's life is on stage. He lives hundred times on stage and dies thousand times on stage. For Dick Shawa it was once in a life time. Stage was his only love and he died in the arms of his beloved. Shawa was a famous comedian and stage actor. One day while performing on the stage in California he fell down and did not get up for quite some time. The audience thought it to be a part of his performance. It was only when the actor's son called out for any doctor from the audience that they realised that Dick was actually sick. Later, doctor's investigations revealed that Dick died of heart attack. (*Times of India*)

Everyone, as a rule, eats to live and sleeps to wake up. But there are exceptions who live to sleep, eat to sleep and finally die in sleep. One such example is of Duke Louigi II (1402-1465) of Savoy. He spent his last 20 years of his life sleeping. He slept for 22 hours a day. The rest of the 2 hours while he was awake were spent in eating. He woke up only three times for breakfast, lunch and dinner and then went back to sleep. He died in his sleep. (*Ripley*)

In 1631, Francois Waltier used antimoni powder for the first time in medical science. The discovery was a landmark in the medical world and was very much appreciated. Dr Waltier was so much influenced with his discovery that he started using this powder in each and every medicine. He died of antimoni poisoning in 1652. (*Ripley*)

There have been several hair-raising stories which could scare one to no end. But this hair-raising story is about hair raising itself. Pierremassy of France could make his hair stand whenever he desired. He was so skilled in that art that he could even make hair on one side of his head stand, whereas the hair on the other half remained down. (*Navbharat Times*)

AIDS is the most dreaded disease of modern times. People would go to any lengths to get a cure for AIDS. When they heard about a lady living in Masaka village in South West of Uganda, who claimed to have a treatment for AIDS; crowds gathered at her doorsteps. People from all over the world queued in front of her house. More than 20,000 people have been said to have taken this miraculous medicine which, in fact, is nothing but soiled water. (*Times of India*)

Porifiria is another rare disease in which the patient is allergic to sun rays. He prefers darkness. His skin becomes dark and the whole body is covered with dark patches. He starts growing hair on the forehead and cheeks. In an advanced form of the disease — Congenial Erythropiatic Porifiria — the victim becomes a blood hound. He starts passing pink coloured urine. His hands lose their shape and change into claws with nails inverted. The description fits into our imaginary Dracula stories. But this is no imaginary Dracula. This is a once normal human being who is now suffering from Porifiria — a rare disease. Till date only 100 such patients are known in the world. (*Balhans*)

In his book *Archives of Anthropology*, Borotels wrote about 'Nialm Nialms' tribe of Africa. He discovered that there were several people in that tribe who had 2-10 inches long tails. According to him among the 116 persons with tails he surveyed, 76 were men and 40 women. Another report from East Indies proves Borotels' tale of tails. Many East Indians were reported to have tails. Special chairs and benches with holes were made for them. The holes were made for their tails so that they could sit comfortably with their tails fitted in it. (*Balhans*)

Breathing is a natural process. However, it was not easy for Rosana Benzi of Italy who suffered a paralytic stroke at the tender age of 14. Due to lungs failure, she had difficulty in breathing. For the next 29 years, she breathed through artificial lungs made of steel. (*Rajasthan Patrika*)

With the increasing inflation, all over the world, it is becoming difficult to make both ends meet. But six-year-old Thyagarajan of Malaysia is proving to be the most expensive child for his parents. Thyagarajan feeds on petrol. He almost behaves like an automobile which runs on petrol. As the car stops functioning when its tank is empty, similarly, if Thyagarajan has not had his share of petrol he would be irritable and refuse to do anything. Doctor's examination, however, declares him a normal healthy child. (*Times of India*)

In 1907, James Thompson of Clair (North Ireland) got up from his bed after 29 years. He was suffering from Chronic Lethargy. Chronic Lethargy is a disease which has no treatment. Even electric shocks have proved ineffective in this disease. Thompson had this attack of Chronic Lethargy in 1877 and since then he was bed-ridden. All these years, his mother tended to his every need. Now when his 80-year-old mother could no longer look after him, Thompson had no choice. (*The Hindu*)

Spending a few days in a hospital is an experience in itself. Martha Nelson of USA spent not just a few weeks or a few months or a few years but a full century (100 years) in the Columbus State Institute of Feeble Minded, Ohio. She was admitted at the institute in 1857 when she was 3-year-old. (*Hindustan Times*)

Cutus Hyper Plastica is a skin disease in which the Patient's skin turns so much elastic that it can be stretched up to one foot and then go back to its original shape.

Gan Keng Woon of Malaysia met with his death while he was playing badminton. During the game, thirty-three-year-old Woon suddenly slipped and fell down. With the jolt, his artificial denture slipped from its place and got stuck in the bronchial tube. By the time he was taken to the hospital, he had died of suffocation. (*Mirror*)

Periodic Insomnia is a disease. In this disease the patient sleeps for weeks together and then he is awake for the next few weeks. Day and night have no significance for them. Their day is the period when they are awake and the night is when they are asleep. During the waking period, they are absolutely normal but while sleeping their diet increases and they suffer from some mental disturbance. Looking at the symptoms of periodic insomnia, it is quite possible that Kumbhkarna of Ramayana was no miracle who suffered form this disease. (*Hindustan Times*)

Water is essential for life. It is unimaginable how anyone can be allergic to it. But it is true. Fifty-five-year-old Stoj Kovic of Yugoslavia is one such person who is suffering from Aquagene Pruritus. Leave alone the bathing, he can't even drink water. For bathing and drinking he uses only alcohol. Do we hear all alcohol-lovers praying for this disease?

(*Times of India*)

Arch Meximenco was a soldier in Second World War. During the war, he lost his speech and hearing power. One day, he saw a dream that he was back into the warfields. The Nazi tanks and soldiers were marching towards him. He saw that he was standing there all alone, unarmed, with no one to help him. Even in such a helpless state, he did not lose heart and set about to fight. Just then, he woke up from his dream and it was like waking up into a new world. He was overcome with joy. He had got his speech and hearing power back. His tension and mental pressure cured him in such a way that no doctor could ever imagine.

Synosis is a heart disease which occurs in infants. The patients of this disease are born with different coloured pigments in their skin. One such boy was born in France. His name was Jewf. His body was covered with different colours by birth. These colours were so dark and natural that they gave the impression of a coloured cloth. Though a brilliant boy, he could only survive for 11 years.

■■

Made in heaven

January 17, 1985 marked the celebration of the wedding of photographer Bruno J. Zehnder with actress Heather May. It was different from others as it took place in an icy cave of Antarctica. Apart from the close friends and relatives who flew down specially for the occasion there were some uninvited guests also — the Penguins. The President of Argentina gave his blessings to the young couple by allowing them to get married at Antarctica.(*Guinness Book*)

In Royal Commission's Report (1986) it was found that till 12th century, 9 out of 10 brides in Scotland were pregnant at the time of their marriage.
(*Strange Stories*)

Can a poor, helpless mouse be responsible for somebody's getting a bride. Unbelievable, but true. A law has been passed at Susukan district in West Jawa. According to the law, no boy can get married until and unless he kills 50 mice and brings them as evidence. This law was passed in the wake of controlling the increasing population of mice in the area.
(*Times of India*)

Mc Peak of Las Vagas was a stunt artist. When he decided to marry Carly, he wanted to have a special wedding: something different. He got married on the Hooverdam at Newas. He carried Carlie on his back and crossed the dam on a 1620 m long, thin wire tied across the river. While keeping his balanace he managed to pronounce the marriage vows with the help of a radio intercom. (*Guinness Book*)

Alfio and Marina Fontana were members of Italian Parachute Acrobatic Team. Together they jumped from 25,000 m and performed some acrobats in the sky. Their flight landed them in a church where their friends and relatives were waiting for them. The two got married in a simple ceremony. (*Times of India*)

God bless Graham Bell — for if he had not invented telephone, Robert Smith could not have married his long-time beloved. Smith was a sergeant in the American Navy. Most of the time he was out of the country. His fiancee got fed up of waiting and gave him an ultimatum. At that time, Smith was posted near Israel. He booked an international call to a Church in Virginia. The two lovers got married over the telephone. (*Times of India*)

Getting married to the people of your own sex is no more a taboo. Denmark, Philippines and many other countries have accepted such marriages and given them a legal status.

In 1970, Diliogen Spings Madwid and Janis Cutler decided to get married in a unique way. They planned an underwater wedding. The priest and a few invitees went 6 m below into the water in a submarine. The bride and the groom jumped into the water in their diving suits. In front of the submarine, with everyone watching from inside, they pronounced their marriage vows. (*Meri Saheli*)

Love never dies. Anne Marie Bernicot was madly in love with Pierre Jean Camon. Their wedding was fixed for the last week of May, 1989. Unfortunately Pierre died on 22 May 1989, a few days before the wedding. Anne Marie was heartbroken. Nevertheless she decided to get married to dead body of Pierre. After obtaining special permission from the Mayor Jean Gaston, the wedding took place at the church. Twenty-four hours after the marriage, Anne Marie was declared widow.

(*The Hindu*)

Michael Mecoy was imprisoned for 26 years. He was charged with a case of dacoity at London on 26 November, 1983. His girl-friend Kathleen did not lose heart and decided to go ahead with their wedding plans. They got married through the bars of prison. It was another thing that as soon as the visiting hours were over the new bride had to return home without the bridegroom. (*Times of India*)

Were they attending a wedding or a funeral? When Georgio Ventura of Italy decided to go to the Church, on a bier, for his marriage, people did not know whether they should celebrate the wedding or mourn it. Even the bride was dressed in black clothes with a garland of Chrysmanthium in her hands (flowers used for funerals). (*Times of India*)

Louis Pasteur, the great scientist was so much devoted to his work that he even forgot his wedding day. On the fateful day, the bride, her family, the priest; even Pasteur's family reached the church in time for the wedding. But the groom was nowhere to be seen. They waited, and waited; all in vain. Worried, they all went in search of Louis who could only be found in his laboratory. (*Vigyan Pragati*)

All is fair in love and war. The Choriti and Chacko tribes of Agve have a strange tradition. If two girls of the tribe fall in love with the same boy, they do not solve their dispute by mere talks. With gloves in their hands they go in for a boxing competition while the boy remains a silent spectator. The winner gets the groom. (*Strange Stories*)

Love knows no bounds of caste and age. Beunus Ayers of Argentina was a 22-year-old young man. One day he went to meet his girl-friend Pantho Sogusa at her house. Incidentally, Pantho's 80-year-old grandmother had come down to visit her the same day. Beunus was so much impressed with the old lady, that instead of the granddaughter he proposed to the granny. Surprisingly, the granny accepted the proposal and they got married.

Marriages are made in heaven. Could it be possible that Lewigir and Winnigir were destined to marry each other twice. For four years, the couple stayed together. Then they divorced each other. Both Lewigir and Winnigir spent the next sixty years married to someone else. In 1978, they reunited and got married for the second time.

Assentus Ogwella of Kenya is 60 years old. He married 125 times. His first marriage took place when he was 19 years old. Since then, he has divorced 85 wives. As per the Leon tribe's rules, each marriage costs Rs. 25,000. Till date Ogwella has spent 25 lakhs on his marriages. Ogwella has 64 sons, 65 daughters and 160 grandchildren.

(*Rajasthan Patrika*)

Number 8 is considered an auspicious number in many countries. Therefore 8.8.88 became an auspicious day for marriages. In Germany, the registration for marriages on this date were mounting high when a young lad rang up with a strange request. He said, 'Though I have not yet selected the bride, the date for the marriage is fixed. Please register my wedding for 8.8.88.' (*Times of India*)

This is the age of computers — two computer freaks proved it by getting married through computer network. Rozen Dedraford and Joe Malakia lived in Mount Bernon. They contacted a priest in New York who gave his consent for their marriage. Two huge computer terminals were set up in both the cities. The priest read the marriage vows to the couple from the New York terminal. The couple in Mount Bernon repeated them from their terminal. The priest conducted the whole ceremony through the computer while the couple in Mount Bernon stood in front of their computer terminal and did as they were told. (*Times of India*)

Sixty-one-year old Naval officer Jim Crowford was in love with Dorothy Ebright. They got engaged. Before the marriage could take place, Dorothy put a condition that she would not marry Crowford until he did something about his snoring. Crowford was operated and finally Dorothy married him with no fear of snores to spoil their honeymoon.

(*Times of India*)

Scales of justice

About 900 km away from Tokyo is Fukoka city. In 1976, the residents of Fukoka filed a suit against the Japanese government. Their petition said that since the aeroplanes landed at the city airport at all odd hours, it disturbed their sleep. This resulted into many problems such as loss of hearing and insomnia. Even their radio and television programmes were disturbed. The case went on for 12 years. Finally the court decided that since the government cannot stop the landing and departure of the planes, it will have to pay the fine to the inhabitants. The Japanese government paid 1.59 million dollars to the residents of Fukoka. (*Times of India*)

Pamella Micthell of America worked with Marriot Corporation, a famous chain of hotels. She kept her hair in 'Cornrow style'. She was more angry than surprised when her employers asked her to either change her hair-style or leave the job. She filed a suit against them. Later on, the hoteliers had to pay 40,000 dollars to settle the case. (*Times of India*)

In Portland, Mrs and Mr Steve Green were travelling in their 1980 model Ford Pinto. On the way, they met with an accident. Their car was hit by a horse carriage. The jolt was so strong that the horse was thrown up in the air and it landed on the roof of the Green's car. The sheet of the roof proved so light that it broke, and Mrs Green died. Mr Green held the Ford Company responsible for his wife's death and took them to court. The Ford Company had to pay 1.5 million dollars' penalty to Mr Green.

(*Times of India*)

This incident occured in California. For a small printing mistake, a telephone company had to pay 10 million dollars to a travel agency. The said travel agency gave an advertisement in the telephone directory. While the original caption said, 'We arrange EXOTIC tours', by mistake it got printed as 'We arrange EROTIC tours'. The travel agency filed the suit against the telephone company with the plea that this advertisement would affect their business by giving them a bad name.

(*Times of India*)

Vicky Ann Guest was an 18 year old student. She wanted to join her school's cheer leading team. But the school authorities declined her request saying that her breasts were too heavy. She should make them smaller by surgery. Vicky filed a case of defamation against the authorities for 1 lakh dollar. Later, they reached an out of court settlement.

(*Times of India*)

The Hollywood actress, Jennifer Leigh, filed a case against her hair dresser for negligence. Jennifer claimed that she had asked Louis Licari to dye her hair in platinum colour, but she, out of sheer negligence, dyed them in a permanent pink colour. (*Times of India*)

Not all animals are as helpless as Master Teddy was. The female elephant in Jaipur along with her Mahaut Chhuttan Khan got hurt in an accident with a State Transport bus near Jalmahal. She herself went to the court to collect the cheque against her claim. The Rajasthan High Court judge handed the cheque for Rs. 21,000/- to the elephant.

(*Rajasthan Patrika*)

Floren Philips of London, a 87-year-old widow was charged by her neighbour Sedra Davis for snoring. Sedra claimed that Floren snored so loudly that Sedras 71-year-old husband, who was a heart patient, could not sleep in peace.

In Norway, when a soldier reported on duty with his pierced ears adorned with earrings, his officer strictly ordered him to take them off. The soldier sued the officer. The local court gave its verdict in his favour saying that since men and women are equal; men have every right to wear earrings like women. (*Times of India*)

A Chinese woman Jheng had an abortion in 1983, after which for many years she could not conceive. When she went to a doctor for check up, she was astonished to find that she was unable to conceive because of the IUD. Later on, it was discovered that after Jheng's abortion, the doctor at the hospital planted an IUD in her uterus without her knowledge. Jheng filed a suit for the penalty of 3000 Yuan. (*Times of India*)

In 1974, Virginia O' Hare of New York contacted plastic surgeon Hark Ballin for plastic surgery of her abdomen to make it look more sexy. The lady had faith in Dr Ballin as she had her nose operated by him a few years ago. Unfortunately this time the doctor goofed. After the operation, Virginia's naval slipped 2 inches backwards from the centre. The doctor re-operated but it was still half an inch short. Virginia filed a suit against the doctor. She won the case and the court ordered the doctor to pay her 1 lakh dollar as penalty; 4,219 dollars for undergoing so much pain and 7.5 lakh dollars to compensate for her professional losses. Later, however, they reached an out of court settlement and the doctor gave her 2 lakh dollars.

When Master Teddy got 2 lakh dollars in his master's will, many people did not like it. It was also mentioned in the will that only after the death of Master Teddy this amount shall be distributed among the relatives. The relatives went to the court with the appeal that they could not wait for the dog to die and the money should be distributed now. But the judge dismissed their petition. Considering the safety of Master Teddy, he also ordered to keep a record of the dog's photographs, etc. so that no one could cheat on the poor animal's legacy. (*Times of India*)

A case of negligence was filed on a hospital by Sandra Ewagen. Sandra was undergoing a treatment for cancer for the last 7 years. She was shocked, when she discovered one day that she never had cancer. In fact, the sample of her healthy tissue got mixed up with a cancer patient in the pathology laboratory. Sandra received 1.55 million pounds as compensation from the hospital. (*The Hindu*)

Sometimes one careless mistake may make you pay heavily. A newly married couple in Japan went on their honeymoon. One day they got so busy in taking that they did not realise when their suitcase slipped away and fell on a doctor sitting below. The doctor got badly hurt and had to take four month's leave from work. He filed a suit against the young couple. Ultimately, the couple had to pay 2,07,800 dollars to the doctor.

A court case which was going on for the last 761 years ended on 28 April, 1966 at Pune. In 1205, Maloji Thorat filed a case claiming his right to have religious public gatherings on festivals. After 761 years this case ended in his favour. Bala Saheb Patilji Thorat heard the verdict on behalf of his ancestor.

It is said that the punishment for one murder is the same as for two or three murders. But 40-year-old Dudley Van Kamzer proved it wrong when he received imprisonment for 10,000 years. The court of Tuskelusey, Alabama gave him this punishment for the three murders he committed in 1976.

The thieves

A man entered the British Home Stores — a large departmental store in London. Quietly he picked up many things, thinking no one is watching him. Hiding them in his clothes just as he was about to leave the store, 8 persons caught him red-handed. In fact, the poor chap had chosen a wrong time for his work. At that time, a meeting of eight detectives was going on in the store.

(*Amazing Blunders*)

Around the world in eight dollars! But William Cohen of Florida did not spend even a single penny for his round the world trip in 1982. Cohen always dreamt of going on a world trip but he had no money to materialise his dream. So he did this — somehow, from somewhere, he got hold of uniform of a flight attendant of airline. When he entered the aircraft at Miami airport, clad in that uniform, nobody paid him much attention. Inside the plane, Cohen started serving drinks efficiently. The passengers

took him to be one of the flight attendants whereas the plane crew passed him off as a replacement for one of their permanent employees. Cohen got down at London; went to all the places he always wanted to see; and returned home using the same trick. He did this many times and without paying even a single penny he visited several places around the world. But every dog has its day. One day the airline received a letter from one of its passengers recommending Cohen for a promotion as he was a very efficient and hard worker. On checking their list of employees the authorities realised that no flight attendant with this name worked with their airline. The next time when Cohen boarded a plane, he was caught red-handed. (*Amazing Blunders*)

Some people are so clumsy — they are all fingers and thumbs. Carlo Colandi of Milan (Italy) was one of them. Once he went on a bank dacoity mission. He parked his car outside the bank. In an attempt to cover his half face Carlo pulled his scarf up as he entered the bank. As soon as he stepped in, he lost his balance and fell down. Embarrassed, he got up and

started to run towards the cashier with a pistol in his hand. Again he slipped on the way. While he was struggling to keep his balance the trigger got pressed and the pistol shot at the ceiling. It looked more like a circus show than a bank robbery. The people found it so funny that they could not control their laughter. Mortified, Carlo retreated and ran towards his car only to find the police waiting for him there. He had parked his car in the 'No Parking' zone. (*Amazing Blunders*)

In 1922, the New York police caught a blind thief. His blindness helped him in recognising things by touching. Since he did not require any light, most of the time he got away unnoticed. (*Amazing Blunders*)

Fifty-four-year old Kenneth Sek of Port Adelaide was caught by the police when he was stealing some books from a local bookshop. A search of his house revealed that he was in this stealing business for a long time. The search party recovered 12 tons of books from his house costing more than 4 lakh American dollars. (*Amazing Blunders*)

In West Germany, the police was chasing a man who ran away after shop-lifting. When the thief came to a dead end, he jumped over the wall, but regretted his act immediately because he had jumped straight into the mouth of the dragon. He was standing in the Dusseldorf prison. The poor man had no choice but to surrender. (*Amazing Blunders*)

The Mez (East France) police arrested a man who used to steal only ladies' clothes from the local laundries. He had a collection of 699 panties, 460 bras, 178 petticoats and many other ladies clothes worth 50,000 francs. (*Amazing Blunders*)

In 1920, five persons were caught by North Carolina police for gambling. When they were brought to the court, the judge punished them in a unique way. He asked the culprits to set their own punishments through gambling. He handed them a dice. Each got imprisonment for as many months as was the number on the dice. The most unfortunate was the one who got two times sixes: the highest number in the game, but most undesirable at that time. (*Amazing Blunders*)

Tattooing may be in fashion, but they can give a person away easily. In Kentucky (USA) a man robbed a bank. He was wearing a mask so that no one could recognise him. But a slight mistake on his part gave him away. It was a hot summer day. To escape the heat, he pulled up his shirt sleeves. He totally forgot about the tattoo on his arm. It was not very difficult for the police to find him with such an easy clue. (*Amazing Blunders*)

Out of the frying pan into the fire. Thomas Gee had already spent two months out of his 12 months' imprisonment, when, one day he chanced upon an opportunity to run away from the prison. It was through the delivery van which came into the prison compound to deliver the vegetables. Quietly Thomas-gee hid under the truck. When the truck left the premises uneventully, Thomas-gee thanked his stars — but not for long. When the truck stopped at its next destination; an oil soaked Thomas-gee came out from underneath. The poor chap did not know whether to laugh or cry at his luck. He was standing in the compound of another prison. The van, in fact, was a supply van which supplied vegetables to all the prisons. (*Amazing Blunders*)

A group of 50 prisoners in Mexico planned an escape. Secretly they started digging a tunnel in the premises. They almost succeeded in their plan except for the fact that they could not measure the length of the tunnel correctly. The tunnel opened into a court room. Everyone in the court was dumbfounded when they recognised these unexpected visitors. The judge, who was passing the judgement on another case, settled this case also then and thereby sending the prisoners back into the jail for a longer period of time. (*Amazing Blunders*)

Bad habits die hard. Else Haffner of Sweden was brought before the magistrate under the charge of burglaries. Since Else was pregnant, the judge freed her with a warning to stay at home and not to indulge in such activities. No sooner the lady left the courtroom she was brought back under a new charge. She had stolen the judge's new fur coat.

(*Greatest Crooks*)

It requires guts to attempt a robbery inside the jail. Two thieves stole two television sets from a prison at Tel Aviv. They cut the prison fence and crossed it with the two television sets. (*Times of India*)

Tit for tat. In an amazing incident at England, two thieves got a dose of their own medicine. While these two thieves were busy robbing a house, the owner of the house came by. After realising the gravity of the situation, instead of calling out for help, which he was sure could not reach in time, he went towards their (the thieves') car which was parked nearby and ran away. Later on, the police estimated that the cost of the car was 1000 pounds whereas the burglary in the farmer's house was not more than 500 pounds. (*Amazing Blunders*)

The Venezuela police issued a warrant in the name of a notorious criminal. When they reached his house to arrest him, a new situation faced them. The criminal's house was situated on the border of Venezuela and Columbia. Half of the house came into Venezuela and the rest was in Columbia. On seeing the police party approaching, the criminal ran towards his bedroom, which came under Columbian border. Since the crime he had committed, was not punishable in Columbia, the lucky fellow escaped. The Venezuela police had to go back empty-handed. (*Greatest Crooks*)

The rolling stones

An amazing incident took place at the Holy Trinity Catholic Church in Petersberg. There is a 60-year-old statue of Jesus Christ in this church. Every year thousands of devotees go there on Good Friday. In 1989, the people watched in amazement when the eyes of this statue closed in front of thousands of people. There were many stories and several explanations for the event, but the real cause is yet to be found. (*Dharmyug*)

The Ires rock of Australia changes its colour throughout the day. This rock is made up of Conglo Meret. Its original colour is red. As the sun changes its direction, the colour of the rock also changes. Sometimes it looks yellow, sometimes purple or red and so on. (*Rajasthan Patrika*)

We have all heard of crocodile tears; ever heard of stone tears? In the Greek Orthodox Church, situated at New York, is a statue which sheds real tears. Thousands of people from all over the world go there to witness this amazing scene. Every request for finding the statue's source of water has been declined by the St. Irin Christovlent Cathedral authorities. Meanwhile, the statue continues to shed tears — a mystery yet to be solved. (*The Hindu*)

Chamiyara Casa village is situated 18 km. from Katra (Jammu). This village is famous for its ancient Casa Rasayani Cave. In the centre of this cave is the Dhansar Pond consisting of a number of stones weighing up to 2 kg. each. The amazing thing is that these heavy stones do not sink into the water despite their weight. They can be seen floating freely in the pond. These stones remind us of the story of Ramayana when Rama built a floating bridge which had no support from beneath. He must have built the bridge by joining this kind of stones together. (*Rajasthan Patrika*)

Yakutsk is a city in Russia. There is a place near Yakutsk which is famous for its weeping rocks. These rocks are situated near Lena river and they are like a long chain of pillars. The crusty surface of these rocks is always covered with tiny water droplets irrespective of the weather. After doing an extensive research on these rocks, the experts have reached the conclusion that these water droplets come from the moisture in the air.

(*Soviet Sangh*)

The musical stones are found in Ambikapur district of Madhya Pradesh. Though the area is full of stones, there are some big stones which sound like metal. The local people call them 'tuntunia stones'. Some people tried to take these stones away but once separated from their roots, they turned into ordinary stones and sounded like ordinary stones. The scientists believe that behind this mystery lies the different structure and air pressure of the rock. (*Balhans*)

The Musical Rocks are found near Rhine river in Germany. These rocks are named after Lorreli, a girl with golden hair. People believe that Lorreli sings in these rocks. Her music attracts the ships. On reaching Lorreli rocks, most of the ships sink. (*Clavine Bumper Book*)

In another one of nature's amazing wonders, the death valley of California still has some rocks which move by themselves. The traces of their movement can be found on the sand. Though the residents of the area call them 'Race Track Rocks', the reason for their movement is yet to be discovered. (*Clavine Bumper Book*)

Much before the man built moving restaurants the nature made a whole moving village. The 'Grassmien village' in Australia is like a small moving hotel for the tourists. It keeps on changing its place. It is said that in the base of the village lies a 100 ft. thick salty rock which is responsible for its movements. (*Rajasthan Patrika*)

Chance

A.D. Jordan of Pennsylvania has insured his house with all its furniture and other things against fire, except his sewing machine. It was a coincidence that twice his house was destroyed in fire. Both the times it was a Saturday. The same person called the fire brigade on both the occasions. It was the same fire brigade company which came to the rescue. On both the days Mrs and Mr Jordan were not at home and surprisingly each time their house was totally destroyed in the fire. All the furniture and other belongings gutted in the fire except the one sewing machine which survived each time.

(*Ripley*)

Othello was the first French life-saving boat. On 4 December 1872, it set out towards its first target and saved an American ship from sinking. It

was a mere coincidence that the rescuer and the rescued shared the same name — Othello.

They had to be tagged as Irin Smith I and Irin Smith II since there was no other way to identify them. On 10 June 1951, two women having the same name — Irin Smith — were admitted to St. Joseph Hospital at Tempa, Florida. Both the ladies were 47-year-old and had to undergo the same kind of operation. It was a strange coincidence that the names of their husbands were also the same — Frank Smith.

There are several amazing coincidences between the two Presidents of America, Abraham Lincoln and Kennedy. Abraham Lincoln was elected President in 1860 and Kennedy was elected in 1960, exactly 100 years later. Lincoln was blessed with two sons, Edward and Robert. Edward died when he was only 3 years old. Kennedy too had two sons named Robert and Edward, out of which Robert died but Edward survived. Lincoln's assistant's name was Kennedy and Kennedy's assistant's name was Lincoln. Both the Presidents were assassinated. They were shot from the back. Both were with their wives when they were shot at. Both died on a Friday. Lincoln was killed in a theatre and his assassin was found in a godown whereas Kennedy was shot from a godown and his assassin was caught in a theater. Both the culprits' names spelled with 15 letters and they were both killed before they could be brought for the trial. Andrew Johnson was Lincoln's successor and was born in 1808. Kennedy's successor was Lindon Johnson who was born in 1908. Both Johnson's names spelled with 13 letters. (*Ripley*)

Albert Einstien and Ottohen were born on the same day — 14 March 1879. Both Einstien and Ottohen won Nobel Prize in their respective fields.

Anyone with the name Hugh Williams can cross the Irish sea without any fear. On 5 December, 1664 a boat sank in Irish ocean, only one passenger out of the 81 passengers survived — his name was Hugh Williams. 121 years later the same incident was repeated with only one person out of 60 passengers surviving. It was Hugh Williams. After 35 years, another ship ssnk at the same place. Again only one man survived out of the 25 passengers. His name was also Hugh Williams.

John Coffy of Ireland did not know that he was digging his own grave when he took charge of the construction of a prison in Dundalk. He was declared bankrupt after some time. John became the first one to occupy this prison. (*Ripley*)

Eighteen was his lucky number. Henry Longfellow wrote 18 books of poetry. He got married at the age of 18. For 18 years he was a professor at Howard University. He died on 18 March 1882.

The meaning of Siat Satiambo is 7 September. When the first child in the family of Siat Satiambol was born on 7 September, 1749 they named him Siat Satiambo. He died on 7 September, 1801. His son was also born on 7 September. He named him Siat Satiambo II. he also died on 7 September. Siat Satiambo III, the grandson too was born on 7 September 1814 and died on 7 September 1862.

Arl Lefralf invented world's first anti-fraud machine. The same Arl Lefralf spend his life in a jail. The charge against him was that he was found to be a fraud. (*Repley*)

Jean De La Belle designed a new torture room and named it 'Iron Cage'. It was so small that the prisoner could neither stand straight nor lie down. As the luck would have it – the first inhabitant of this cage was none other than Jean De La Belle. (*Repley*)

Dr. Charles Drew worked in the field of blood and plasma transfusion. His contributions to this field are outstanding. He found out the ways to store the blood and plasma. In this way he saved many lives and his work proved a great help to mankind. But the same Dr. Drew, who saved blood for all, himself died in a road accident in 1950. The cause of his death was excessive bleeding. (*Repley*)

Someone up there loved him, looked after him. Lt. Bohale of German Air Force was on a testing flight in 1917 when this incident occured. Bohale was flying with pilot Rosen Gart. The plane was flying at the height of 1500 ft. when suddenly the engine failed. The jolt threw Bohale out of the plane. Just as the plane started falling from the height, the pilot felt another jolt. On looking back he was astonished to find the Lt. back in his seat. The engine also whirred and the two happily landed to safety.

April 18 is a dreaded day for St. Mularich Church in Germany. Between 1599 to 1783, lightening struck this church four times, everytime on 18 April.

Fritz Hayber invented powerful Nitrate Bombs for Germany. His discovery was of great help to the German during the first World War. During the Second World War Hayber helped Germany in its 'Poison gas Mass Murders'. Hayber was rewarded for his services in the most cruelsome manner. He was shot dead. Hayber was a Jew. (*Repley*)

Daniel Spicer was killed on 5 March, 1784 in Springfield. He was shot by two bullets in his chest which went through his coat leaving two noticeable marks on it. His brother Zavez Spicer picked up where Daniel had left. He led the revolution against Shez. On 25 January 1787, Zavez was also shot dead. At that time, he was wearing the same coat with two holes which his brother had put on at the time of his death. Zavez was also hit by two bullets which went through the same holes.

King Amberton of Italy (1844-1900) was surprised when he came across Ambryerty Santini. Not only Amberty resembled the king but there were other similarities too. Both the king and Amberty were born on the same day. The day Amberton became the king, Amberty became the owner of a restaurant. Their wives also had the same name — Margarita. Both had one son each, named Vittorio. Amberton and Amberty both died on the same day.

(*Repley*)

Ismat Be was another such person who resembled his kin so much that he was mistaken as the king many times. Ismat and the king of Turkey, Abdul Hameed were born on the same day. Many a time when the king was unwell Ismat Be posed as the king to the public. No one recognized him.

Was he lucky or was it a sheer coincidence. Cassimer Palemus of France was the person who survived three ship mishaps. Each time he was the sole survivor. On 11 July 1875 'Geeanne Catherine' ship was wrecked near Brest. On 4 September 1880 'Tramps Fretz' and on 9 January, 1882 'Al Odeon' sunk near New Foundland. All the three ships were destroyed completely. Whatever remained of them was Cassimer Palemus; who escaped unhurt.

Louis Galdy of Portroyal, Jamaica was buried alive in an earthquake on 7 June, 1962. No sooner had he went inside the earth there was another earthquake which split the earth into two. It was only a matter of few seconds before Galdya was back. He lived happily for another 47 years.

It was a 'cursed' engine. It started with 'Zodaviaz' ship. The ship could take only three rounds of Mississippi river when it met with an accident. The engine was retrieved and fitted into a steamboat 'reindeer'. This boat could take only four rounds and went down into the water. The engine was now used in 'Reindeer II'. After four trips to the shore Reindeer II also met the same fate. The engine which was still in perfect condition was now fitted in 'S.S. Munroe' ship. The ship was destroyed in a fire but the engine survived. This time instead of using it in water the engine was brought to land. It was fitted in a flour mill. But the engine was carrying with the same curse. After one year the flour mill closed down.

(*Ripley*)

In 1911, Sir Edmund Berry was killed in Greenberry Hills. the three assassins executed for his murder were Green, Berry and Hill. In other words we can say that Sir Berry was killed by Green, Berry, Hill in Greenberry Hills.

It seems Tenner Eugene Mesole was possessed by some unknown power. Whenever he sang 'O God, Crush him', it literally happened. In 1849, he was singing in an opera at Paris when he pointed towards the ceiling while singing, 'O God, crush him'. A moment later, a labourer

who was sitting there for light adjustments fell down and died. The next day, in the same opera, Tenner was again singing the same line when he pointed towards an empty chair. A few minutes later a man who came and sat down on the chair suddenly fell from the chair and died. Again on the third day when the same show was going on Tenner's finger pointed towards his own orchestra party while he was singing the same line 'O God, crush him' and to everybody's surprise a member of his orchestra team fell to the ground and died.

Japan was hit by sever earthquakes on the following dates. Apart from the same date 1 September, all these years were in odd numbers.

1 September, 827	1 September, 859
1 September, 867	1 September, 1135
1 September, 1649	1 September, 1923

Wlthough it is not such a common name, it was a coincidence that this case involved all the Satpals. Mr. Satpal Manga was as advocate. One day a man approached him to file his case. The name of the client was also Satpal and his case was against another Satpal. When they reached the court they were surprised to note that the opposition lawyer's name was also Satpal. Even the name of the presiding officer was Satpal.

(*Kadambini*)

Carceles Carmadrek town had not witnessed a single incident of fire in the last 20 years. One day the Mayor of this town thought that the Fire Brigade employees might have been bored to death, as they had no work. So, in a generous mood, the Mayor gave all of them the day off and sent them on a picnic. Alas! As soon as they left the town, fire gutted the Mayor's office. (*Amazing Blunders*)

In a cricket match at Melbourne, Australia defeated England by 45 runs in 1877. Hundred years later, in 1977 again Australia defeated England by 45 runs. (*Navbharat Times*)

In 1944, when Allied countries were planning an attack on Normandy, they had set some highly confidential code words. It was a coincidence that all these code words were the answer to a crossword puzzle published in 'Daily Telegraph' newspaper. A school teacher, Leonard Dew, who had no idea of the importance of these words, used them in the puzzle. (*Book of List*)

Home: sweet home

Sarah Winchester built a strange house in California. This house was constructed in 1922 and had 750 rooms. The house had many illusive chimneys, doors and galleries which were only intended to be seen but not used. Sarah built this kind of house with the hope that the ghosts will be lost in it and will not be able to reach him.

(*Children Records*)

Alice Stenman of Pigeen Cove, Massachusetts built a paper house in 1942. It took one lakh newspapers to build this house. The walls, furniture, clock, table, chairs, everything in this house was made of paper.

(*Children Records*)

Glass houses are fragile; paper houses are delicate; bone houses are something different. Irastha tribe of Nigeria build their houses with animal bones. They join these bones with a solution, then put them to dry. After the bones have dried up, they are used for building houses. A 1000-year-old house, made of bones, can still be seen in this village.

(*Hindustan*)

A 9000-year-old village has been discovered in Turkey by the Archeological Survey Department. The village was a kind of its own as it was closed like a bee-hive. It had no roads, lanes or by-lanes. They even had no doors. Their roofs were joined to each other. The only way of moving in and out was through a ladder connecting one roof to the other.

(*The Hindu*)

The world's smallest church is situated in Verona, New York. This church is only 1 × 1.9 m in size. It was built by Shandeler Mason. This Cross Island Church stands in the middle of a pond. Nowadays it is used only for marriages. The church is so small that only bride, bridegroom and one priest can stand inside the church. All the friends and relatives have to wait outside the church. (*The Hindu*)

Huge buildings are being constructed all over the world. But in this field also, Japan is ahead of all. Japanese have planned a building 'AEROPOLIS' in Tokyo city which will have 500 floors. Aeropolis will be spread in 11 lakh square metre area. This building will cost around 333 billion dollars. Instead of elevator, the building will be equipped with shuttle with a capacity of 100 persons per trip. The shuttle will take only one minute to travel from Ist floor to 500th floor. (*Patrika*)

In 1948, Mehlon Henn built a house in York, Pennsylvania. This house was in the form of a shoe thus known as shoehouse. The house measures 7.5 m from heel to the roof and 14.5 m. from heel to the toe. Very soon, American Government plans to include this shoehouse in their list of historical places. (*The Hindu*)

People living in glass houses need not be extra careful anymore. In New York a glass house has been built by Coaching Glass Works company which is 368 ft. tall and has 28 floors all of which are fully occupied. The walls, roof, doors, interior decoration, even the furniture is made of glass. (*Balhans*)

A 'Calender House' was built in 1585 at Kambe, Wales by Royal Cammibarean Academy of Art. The building has 365 windows, 52 doors and 52 stairs.

The Lussera Church of Italy was built by Charles II in 1300. This church was constructed with the remains of an Arabian mosque. It is said that in ancient times a mosque was also built from the remains of another church.

■■

It's a mad, mad world

Maharaja Sawai Mansingh of Bharatpur was a car freak. Once in London, he went into the showroom of Rolls Royce cars. Being a Maharaja, he was so used to getting all the attention from everyone. Here, he was not properly treated or attended by anybody and as such he felt totally insulted being treated as an ordinary customer. In a fit of anger he bought all the three Rolls Royce available in the showroom and started using them as truck pullers with a garbage trailor attached to them.

George Evar of Peru preferred horses to men. So obsessed was he with the horses that he himself started living and behaving like a horse. He nailed his shoes with horshoe, bridled himself and started pulling a horse cart. He even started eating grass.

Playing with dolls is a child's privilege and playing with elephants is a king's. Nawab Aasafaddola arranged his elephant Dalbadal's marriage with Badkani. The Nawab himself went with the 'Barat' with 1200 elephants as 'Barati'.

Lord Raqwi believed that if he immersed his body in salted sea water, his intestines would be stronger. And he did exactly that. Everyday, a procession would start from his residence to the sea shore where Lord Raqwi would spend hours inside the sea water.

One day, a dog was barking in Nawab Gaziuddin Haider's garden. The Nawab did not like the dog's bark and so he asked his courtiers to find a way to keep it quiet. The courtiers suggested that if the dog could be fed everyday on 10 kg 'Gulkand' (pulp of rose leaves) and a bottle of rosewater, it may become sober and stop barking. The king liked the idea and granted his permission. Though the dog died in 1816, two years after this incident, the clever courtiers went on receiving the supply of 'Gulkand' and rosewater till 1850.

William Backford lived alone in his huge mansion at London. Though he never invited anyone to his house, his dinner table was always set for 12 persons. The food was served in all the 12 plates by 12 servants individually. William Backford ate alone on this table. After he finished eating, the rest of the food was sent back.

The Earl VIII of Bridgewater, Francis Henry Agarton was very fond of pets and shoes. He wore new shoes every day. Even his pet dogs had shoes made of the finest leather. The Earl always had his dinner with his pet dogs. The dinner table would be set for 12. Earl and his dogs would enjoy their meals together. If ever, any dog dared to behave like a 'dog' it would be taken away by the servants and would only be brought back after it had learned the 'table manners'.

The flies flee at the mere mention of his name. Mr Hucha has been after their lives for the last 21 years. Hucha, a retired gentleman, kills about 4000 flies everyday. Till date, he has killed more than 17 kg. flies.

The famous industrialist Howard Hughs had a mania to clean his hands. A box of napkins was always kept near him so that he could clean his hands. He spent the last ten years of his life secluded in a hotel room. During this period, only twice he came out to have his nails and hair cut. The secret of Mark Twain's wonderful work is a bathtub. He wrote most of his books, lying in a bathtub. Victor Hugo liked to write in a closed room totally undressed.

Hatty Greene was the richest woman of the world but she lived like the poorest woman. She always wore cheap clothes, lived in a stingy den. She never had a proper hearty meal. She would travel miles just to collect a measley amount. She always travelled by the cheapest means. She left behind more than 200 million dollars when she died at the age of 80. Though she never spared a single penny as charity, after her death, all her money went to a charitable institution.

One day some people in Brest (France) complained about a horrible smell in their neighbourhood. Though it was there for a long time, now it had become intolerable. A thorough search of the area revealed that the smell was coming from a house. When the sanitation officer entered the house, he was astonished to find all the 8 rooms in the house filled with garbage. The 68-year-old lady who lived there all alone, admitted that for the last 18 years she had been storing her garbage in these rooms.

(*Mirror*)

Finally the cats got the cream. Twenty five stray cats could not believe their good luck when the Arabian Prince Mohammad Ali Fassi fell in love with them and brought them to his palace. These cats are now having a whale of a time. They live in a 32 lakh dollar palace, eat their favourite dishes and sleep on thick cushioned mattresses. What's more, the prince plans on spending 25 lakh dollars per annum on these cats.

(*Rajasthan Patrika*)

■■

Comedy of errors

Typing errors are common, but this error cost 2 million dollars to the American Government. A typist was given a letter in which she had to type 'All imported fruit-plants are free from taxes'. She typed it as 'All imported fruit, plants are free from from taxes.' Though the original order was to make only those imported plants tax free which bore fruits, a slight typing error made all the imported plants as well as fruits free from tax. By the time it was rectified the damage was already done.

(Book of List)

Man made flawless computers but he himself is full of errors. Rocket 'Mariner I' was ready for launch on 28 July 1962. The calculations showed that 13 minutes after the rocket left for Jupiter, its speed would

be 25820 miles per hour. 9800 solar cells would open after 44 minutes and 80 minutes later, the computer would set its direction. The count down began and within seconds the rocket was on its way. Just as the scientists were about to celebrate the successful launch of Mariner I, the computer terminals went blank and two minutes later the rocket fell into Atlantic Ocean. Later investigations revealed that while feeding the information in the computer the signs of addition (+) and subtraction (–) were left out. This small mistake cost them a big amount – 18.5 million dollars.

(Book of List)

On 31 December 1986 millions of Germans were glued to their TV sets to listen to the speech of their Chancellor Herr Von Weizsaecker. When the speech began, many people felt as if they had already heard this speech before. In fact, it was the same speech which was given by the Chancellor, the previous year, on 31 December 1985. Later the television authorities apologised for having played the old cassettes by mistake.

(Amazing Blunders)

In Frankfurt, some labourers locked themselves inside a building. it so happened, that while constructing the building they sealed the only entrance of the building with concrete. Later on, they were rescued through a ventilator. *(Clavine Bumber Book)*

Larry Walers tied 42 balloons on his easy chair and off he went, free as a bird, in the vast sky. He flew up to 3 miles. During his flight, many aeroplanes passed by, many birds fluttered around him; all astonished to see this strange rider. After some time when he came down, it was Larry's turn to be surprised when he found the traffic police waiting for him there. Larry was arrested. He had committed the blunder of not taking the licence to fly.

(Amazing Blunders)

In 1840, a waterway was planned in Western Ireland between Corib and Musk lakes. To begin with, they put a thick layer of porous Calcium Carbonate but when they released water in it all the water went inside the earth. They tried other means to retain the water. Later on, when the construction work was almost over, they discovered, that the height of both the lakes was different from the sea level. Now they realised that they were trying to perform an impossible task by making the water flow in opposite direction i.e., from lower slope to the higher. All the money and labour of so many years went down the drain. *(Book of Facts)*

In 1979, he temperature outside was below freezing point, when Peter Rowlands tried to open his car door. When he tried to insert the key, he realised that the hole was covered with snow. In an attempt to melt the snow he started blowing. Larry panicked when he found his lips stuck to the ice. Poor chap had to stand for 20 minutes in severe cold with his lips sealed,till someone came to his rescue. *(Amazing Blunders)*

In 1985, the United Nations Organisation decided to celebrate their 40th Anniversary by sending an expedition to Mount Everest. However, the group could not succeed in their mission due to the bad weather. So they hoisted UNO flag 800 ft. below the Mount Everest and that too upside down. A group photograph revealed this mistake later. By then it was too late. *(Amazing Blunders)*

In 1978, at Chesterfield, in England the cleaning work of Stockwith canal was in progress. This canal is more than 200 years old. The workers did not know that there was metal plug somewhere in the middle of the canal which was the key factor for the existence of the canal. By mistake, this plug got removed from its place. The people watched in amazement as all the water went through this hole leaving their boats sailing on dry land. They had to cross the canal by foot. *(Amazing Blunders)*

‘Either you employ tall postmen or put me down’. A poor letter box complained at Ballymacra County, Ireland in March 1979. This letter box got stuck 9 ft. above the ground on a pillar when the old pillars were being replaced by the new ones.

(Amazing Blunders)

It was a minor accident when a 30 cents’ can-opener fell into the Torpedo-throwing-machine of an American Atomic submarine in September 1978. But the cost involved in repairing this machine was not that small – it was 1,71,000 dollars.

(Book of List)

The Royal Society for the Prevention of Accidents had set up an exhibition at Harrogate, London in 1968. Which had to be closed down much before its closing date — due to an accident. *(Amazing Blunders)*

A plastic token worth not more than 2 cents was on display at a museum in Southshieds in England alongwith precious rare coins. This plastic coin had ‘R’ written in Roman style. The experts claimed it belonging to the period A.D. 135-138. But a small girl, Fiona Gorden could not be convinced by any explanation. She insisted that this was a plastic token of a soft drink company and the ‘R’ inscribed on the coin was the first letter of the soft drink producer’s name. A closer look at the alleged coin confirmed the girl’s story. The coin actually belonged to the 20th century.

(Amazing Blunders)

Alceo Dossena was an expert at copying statues. In 1927, America's Cleveland Museum of Art received a shock when they found out that their famous wood carving 'Medonna and Child' was actually a fake. The figure did not belong to 13th century as it claimed to be, instead it was made by Alceo Dossena in 1920. The museum authorities removed it and replaced it with a 120,000 dollars' marble statue of 'Athena'. Little did they know that they were again conned by the same person. Athena was also a fake one made by none other than, Dossena. *(Greatest Crooks)*

A bridge was under construction in Pennsylvania. The bridge was being constructed simultaneously from both the ends and it was to be joined in the middle. Due to some calculation error on part of the engineers, when the time to join the bridge at the midpoint came, it was found that the two ends were still 15 ft. apart. *(Ripley)*

In 1983, a new telephone directory was printed in Paris. The Telecommunications Department took pride in announcing that it was foolproof. They were embarrassed when someone pointed out their biggest mistake ever. The Telecommunications Department's own telephone numbers were all wrongly printed. *(Amazing Blunders)*

The first 'Perfect Book' of the world was published in 1744. The book was read 500 times by 6 proofreaders. The publishers were convinced that it was really a 'Perfect Book' so they announced an award of 250 dollars for pointing out any mistake in the book. The 'Perfect' book proved to be not so perfect. There were six typographical errors, out of which one was in the first line of the first page of the book. *(Ripley)*

One day three men, clad with rifles, set about to rob a post office in Bellericay, Essex in England. When they reached the distination they could not help cursing their luck. The post office, they had set their eyes on, had closed down 12 years ago. *(Amazing Blunders)*

A letter box in West Hungary remained closed for 11 years. Though people continued using it, their letters never reached the destination. This letter box was situated in a hospital at Gyore city. A watchman was responsible for retrieving letters from this letter box and hand over to the Mail Department. In 1978, when his duty changed, no one thought of the letter box; neither the Hospital authorities nor the Mail Department. From 1978 to 1989, patients kept on mailing their letters in this letter box, which was never emptied. It was only when the letter box got cluttered with letters up to the brim that someone noticed it and complained to the concerned authorities. After 11 years, the poor letter box received some attention. *(Times of India)*

Mr. Burleigh of Britain founded the newspaper 'Commonwealth Sentinel'. The paper started with much fanfare. Latest news items, interesting stories, clourful advertisements adorned the paper. Burleigh himself covered most of the articles, arranged for the advertisements and supervised the printing. But there was one area which he forgot to take care of the distribution of the paper. He forgot to arrange for the distributors. Not a single copy could be sold due to this mistake. 6 February 1965 became the first and the last day for the newspaper 'Commonwealth Sentinel'.

(Amazing Blunders)

In World Cup Soccer 1990, Holland was cent per cent sure of its victory. So confident were they, that even before the team won the finals, the overenthusiast officers in Holland got a million postage stamps saying 'Netherland 1991' World Cup Winners printed. Unfortunately, Holland could not win the finals and these one million stamps had to be destroyed.

(The Hindu)

In November, 1918, at the end of First World War, a pact was signed by Allied countries. It was later revealed that some pages of this pact were typed with carbon facing wrong side of the paper, due to which these papers could only be read from back to front. *(Amazing Blunders)*

In an unsuccessful attempt, China tried to copy American Boeing 707 plane. But they forgot to check its centre of gravity. The net result — Chinese Y-10 failed to take off. *(Ripley)*

To connect the Chicago and Illinois cities, the American Government decided to build an underground passage. Since the administrative control of the two cities was in different hands, the order for this tunnel was given to two different masons. Both started work simultaneously from their respective end — one from Chicago and the other from Illinois. When the construction was in the last stage it was found that the two masons had no co-ordination. One tunnel was 23 cm. below from the other and though, according to the engineers, the construction was over, both the tunnels were still 20 cm. apart. The government had t0 bear a loss of 3,09,000 dollars. *(Book of Facts)*

■■

Card game

In 1624, Hotel 'Suli', which was yet to be constructed, was lost by one of the partners in a card game. The bet among the two partners was that the loser will have to bear all the expenses for construction of this hotel. *(Ripley)*

In 1760, Sir, Richard Temple's wife Anne lost 50,000 pounds in a slimy bet. The bet was placed on some worms.

Duchess Mazarin was on her death bed when she played her last hand in a card game. She bet with her partners that whoever lost the game will have to pay for her funeral. As soon as the game finished, the Duchess died. *(Ripley)*

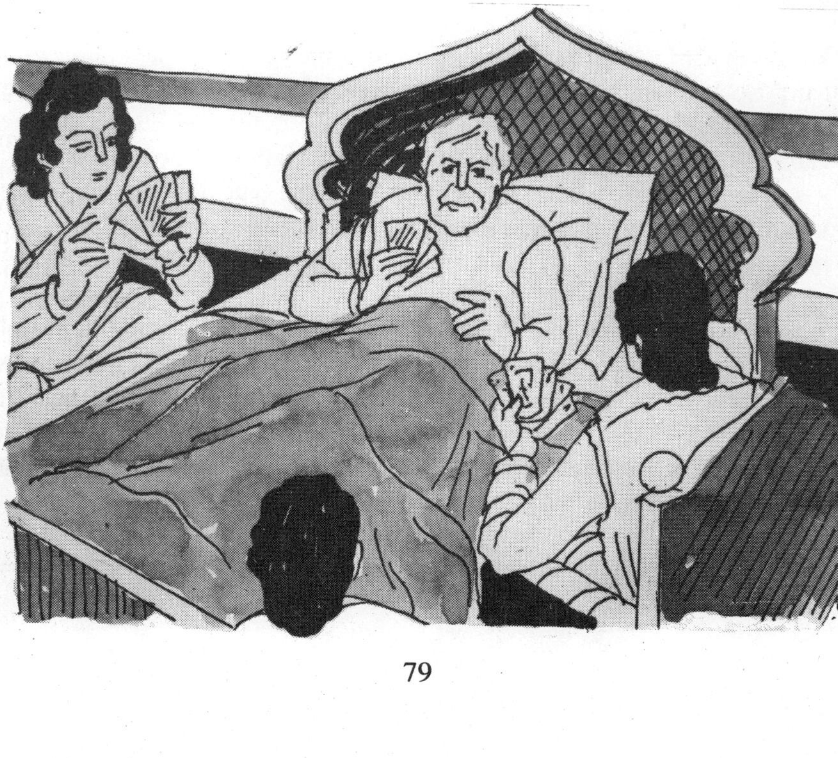

Lord Arlington (1618-1685) once bet 3000 pounds on tiny water droplet on a glass window. The bet was on which of the two drops of water would reach the bottom of a windowpane first. *(Ripley)*

Captain E.M. Kingsbury felt disgusted while he was in the middle of a card game at San Carlos Indian Reserve in Arizona. He had been playing for one hour when his attention shifted to the quality of the cards. The cards were made of a very good quality raw leather. When the Captain asked his host as to where he could get the same type of cards, he started laughing. The truth was that these cards were made from the skin of the prisoners. *(Ripley)*

Governor of Riyadh lost 30 lakh dollars in 3 days while gambling. But it did not seem to bother him at all. Before leaving the hotel he gave tips to all the waitors in his usual royal manner 150 pounds each.

In 1896, when the Olympics had just begun, a Greek millionaire Georgia Gawargios proposed his daughter's hand and a cash award of 193000 dollars to any Greek athlete who won the Marathon race. Though the race was won by a Greek athlete, Spridion Love, he could not fulfil the millionaire's wish, since Spridion Love was already married.

Till some time back, though the gambling was allowed in Monte Carlo, it was only open for the foreigners. No local resident was allowed to enter the casino.

It is the winning that matters, not the money. The Duke of Guise (1519-1563) had bet all his wealth (almost 8 million pounds) on one card, Though the chances of winning were 1/400, luckily he won. The Duke won 20,000 pounds that too he gave away as a tip to the messenger who brought this good news to him. *(Ripley)*

In Las Vagas, gambling is on for 24 hours a day, throughout the year. Only on New Year Eve it stops for half minute at midnight.

Rich man – poor man

It was a chance which comes once in a lifetime. The people of Zagreb town in Yugoslavia found some local and foreign currency in a dustbin. Within seconds huge crowds gathered and people grabbed as many notes as they could. However, the real source of this money remains a mystery. The total value of the currency was more than 600 million Dinars. *(Times of India)*

When Enna's husband died, she was overcome with grief. Later on, as she regained composure and started looking around the house for her husband's savings, she could find none. She knew that her miser husband

was a millionaire. She pleaded with the village authorities to allow her to dig her husband's grave and search his clothes. When the late husband's body was taken out and scanned; Enna found 6 million liras in his watch pocket. *(Times of India)*

The rain uncovered a treasure at the Boajidu village in Sierra Leone. The heavy rain washed away the soil and sparkling diamonds could be seen. The news spread like fire. Within seconds a huge crowd gathered about. The army had to be called to control the situation. *(Times of India)*

Mrs Pearl Andersen of California dreamt one night that lot of money was coming out of a slot machine. Then she woke up. It was past midnight, when she drove up to Newda and tried her luck on slot machine. The dream turned true when Pearl won first prize of one million dollar.

Two persons were collecting sea moss in Honjo, Akita (Japan) when their gaze fell upon a sport bag lying on the sea shore. When they opened it, they gaped in astonishment. The bag was full of money — about 11.4 million yen in cash. The two honest men went to the police station and deposited the bag there. When no one came to collect it for a long time, the bag was handed back to them. *(Times of India)*

Sue Zera lived in Columbia and worked as bartender. One day a customer gave her 50 dollars to buy him 50 lottery tickets of Illinois State Lottery. By mistake, Sue Zera put the money in another machine which gave her different lottery tickets. When she went back with those tickets the customer refused to take them. Sue Zera had no choice but to return his money and somehow dispose of these 50 tickets. She tried to sell them to other customers but could only sell 20 tickets. The rest of the 30 tickets were still with her. She mourned the loss of 30 precious dollars unaware that she was in for a pleasant surprise. Two days later, she became a millionaire. She had won 10 million dollars on one of the tickets.

(Times of India)

Kenneth Lain lived in a rented house in Temele (Arizona). The house was full of cockroaches. One day Kenneth set about to get rid of them. He picked up the repellant and started spraying at every expected hiding place. When he tried to spray behind the air-conditioner, he found an old bag lying there. The bag contained 75000 dollars in cash.

(Times of India)

Grant was a clever business man. In 1861, he made a silk purse out of a sow's ear. When he heard the news of Prince Albert's sickness, he bought all the black crape cloth from the market. When Prince Albert died, his farsightedness paid him dividend. Grant could sell this cloth at a profit of 25 lakh pounds.

Opportunity knocks at your doorstep but this opportunity was lying in a letter box. It was Mrs. Naukiro Yamato's letter box where she found two packets. One was covered with newspaper and the other with a scarf. Suspiciously, she opened it. The packets contained 10 million yen and 24 lakh yen respectively. Since there were no claimants for this money, it was given back to Mrs. Yamato.

The famous millionaire James Gordan Bennett was very fond of mutton chops made in a particular restaurant in Monte Carlo. Every night he would go to the same restaurant, sit at the same table and order the same dish — mutton chops. One day as he went to the restaurant he found someone else sitting on his favourite table. Instead of waiting for the table to be free, Bennett went to the restaurant owner and bought the restaurant for 40,000 dollar. Next he went to the man sitting on his favourite place and asked him to vacate the table. Satisfied Bennett sat down on his table, ordered his favourite dish and before leaving, gave the restaurant to the waiter who had served him that evening — as tip. *(David Frost)*

Gaston Dumerg was the President of France for seven years; from 1924-1931. He could not save any money during this period. In 1931, when he was relieved and he returned to his normal life, Gaston bought a lottery ticket and won 1 lakh dollars.

A Woman in Rhodes island was cleaning her backyard when she discovered a six feet wide secret bracket in a corner built by her late husband. When she opened it she found two tons of silver hidden there.

The Spanish Government gave 9 lakh dollars to the first prize winner of their state lottery. In 1860, Santiago Alanso Cardio won the first prize. But the tragedy was that the government did not have enough cash to pay him. Instead of the cash award, Santiago was presented a huge mansion 'Casse De Cardio' in Madrid.

An old couple bought a bronze statue for 100 pounds and put it in their garden. Thirty years later when they tried to sell it, they were astonished to find that the statue was a rare antique piece made by a famous sculpture of 17th century: Adrine De Waris. A mere 100 pound statue made them millionaire over night.

■■

Raining cats & dogs

It rained knitting needles in Harrodsburg, Kentucky, in March 1856. The reason being a needle factory which was destroyed in a cyclone. The needles had been lifted up by swirling updrafts of air. *(Ripley)*

It rained thousands of birds on May 15, 1942, on the town of Pageland, South Carolina. *(Ripley)*

It rained bullfrogs on Memphis, Tennessee, on 25 October, 1946. *(Ripley)*

It rained with red soil on the Italian Riveria on 23 March, 1937. This rain was the result of clouds of red dust from Africa, swept over the Mediterranean. *(Ripley)*

This was the kind of rain which is everyone's secret dream. On 8 October 1976 an aeroplane passed by Rome, raining Italian liras. Overnight the people in that area became millionaires.

It rained fish near Wales on 11 February 1959.

Haiti had been hit by a severe draught for over six months when suddenly it started raining. It was no ordinary rain. That day black eggs rained from the sky.

A Snowstorm hit the Sahara Desert in February 1979. It was so heavy, it halted the traffic in one town in southern Algeria. *(Ripley)*

Snow fell for the first time in 3000 years on Serir Benaffen and Gargaff, the most arid parts of the Sahara Desert, on 6 January 1913. Four inches of snow turned the hot sands into the cool lands of Antarctica.

(Ripley)

When cats and dogs came down with heavy rains in England, people found another way to describe heavy rains. They called it 'raining cats and dogs'.

Marvels of invention

In an odd coincidence, the first messege transmitted by telephone was a cry for help from its inventor. It was on 10 March 1876. Graham Bell and his assistant Watson were trying out a new liquid transmitter in Exeter Place, Boston. They were in different rooms when Watson suddenly heard the words, 'Mr Watson, come here. I want you.' Bell had spilled some acid on his trousers. A few seconds later Watson burst into the room, saying, 'Mr. bell, I distinctly heard every word you said.' Bells words became the first ever uttered over telephone.

Swiss Chemist Albert Hofmann was investigating a new chemical in 1943 when he absorbed some through his skin and began to hallucinate. He later investigated the strange substance and discovered — LSD.

A gentleman without a hat? But there was a time when wearing a hat was a crime and it could send you to jail. In 1797, when John Hitherigton first invented hat, in his enthusiasm, he went out on the streets of London wearing his newly designed hat. Crowds gathered around him. Dogs started barking. Many women fainted. Police locked him up for trying to scare the public with his horrible head cover.

Someone knocked over a lamp in the home of a French dyemaker in 1825. The fuel removed the stains on the tablecloth... and the drycleaning was invented.

Before fifteenth century the clocks used to have just one arm to tell the hours. No one bothered about the minutes.

Charles Goodyear was working on a stove when he dropped a chunk of rubber gum and piece of sulphur onto the hot stove. The result was an elastic, stable and tough material. It was vulcanized rubber.

In nineteenth century people could wear their shoes without giving them a second look. Both the shoes were the same. They were not different for left and right feet.

German chemist C.F. Schobein disobeyed his wife in 1845 — with explosive results. She had told him to keep his smelly chemicals out of her kitchen but he sneaked in while she was out shopping. There he spilled some acid on her apron. Worried, he hung the apron up to dry over the stove. The result? An explosion. The cellulose in the apron combined with the acid to make nitrocellulose — an explosive that has now replaced gunpowder.

A cat entered a laboratory when someone shooed it away. In its hurry to run, the cat spilled Formaldehyde chemical on a piece of cheese lying there. The chemical reacted with the cheese turning it into hard plastic.

Hoax-n-jokes

In 1835, a geologist Sir John Herschel gave a detailed version of his strange findings in the newspaper *New York Sun*. The geologist claimed to have seen life on moon through a very powerful telescope. Herschel described moon as a fully inhabited planet with lots of vegetation, jungles, animals and human beings. The details were so accurate that many people believed him. The truth came out when a science magazine *Journal of Commerce* contacted the newspaper for their permission to print this news in their magazine. Then the publishers disclosed that it was not a true story and was only meant to be a joke. There was no geologist by that name, the article was written by Richard Adams Lock. *(Amazing Hoaxes)*

Can furs grow on their own ? No! But thousands of readers believed *Daily Express* when it published a special report about the long fur caps

worn by security guards. The British newspaper said in its report that these caps are made of a different kind of fur which grows like hair. From time to time these guards go to barbers and have their fur caps trimmed. Alongwith the feature a photograph was also shown, in which a security guard, wearing his fur cap, was sitting on a chair in a barber shop. The barber was trimming the cap. *(Amazing Hoaxes)*

Abraham Lincoln's favourite joke was about the footprints. He had the ceiling of his room painted with a design of footprints. The idea was anyone entering the room should be shocked to find someone's footprints on the ceiling. Lincoln succeeded in his joke many times, when people were left wondering as to how could anyone walk on the ceiling leaving such clear footprints behind. *(Amazing Hoaxes)*

This incident happened during Vietnam War. The fine day, American President Lyndon Johnson decided to meet the American troops which were on their way to Vietnam. It so happened, that on that fateful day the soldiers had a farewell party. The whole group was dead drunk and was in no condition to meet the President. So, the officers prepared the troop which had just returned from Vietnam and introduced it as the departing team. The President shook hands with them and was so impressed with the soldiers that he decided to stay on till they left for Vietnam. The

officers had no choice except for staging a fake farewell. The poor soldiers had to board the same plane which had just brought them back. After seeing the plane off, the President and his people left. Then only, the plane which was taking rounds in the sky landed and everyone heaved a sigh of relief. *(Amazing Hoaxes)*

Once Churchill was chickened out by Roosevelt. During the Second World War, the British Prime Minister, Winston Churchill and the American President Roosevelt used to discuss serious political matters over the morning breakfast. One day, as usual, they were having their breakfast together. When Churchill opened his boiled egg, to his utter surprise, there came out — a chicken. Later, he discovered that this egg was Rossevelt's idea. He had ordered to empty an egg and put a tiny chicken in it. Almost invisible holes were made in the shell so that the chicken could breathe. The job was done so neatly that, for once, the Prime Minister of Britain was also duped. *(Amazing Hoaxes)*

Fact or fiction? Lama Lobsang Rampa wrote many books about his life at monastery and his sixth sense. Though the people believed him, the fact remained, that there was no such Lama with this name nor was there any such monastery. The books were all fiction written by Syril Henry Hauskins under the pen name Lama Lobsang Rampa .

(Amazing Hoaxes)

■■

Looney laws

During the reign of Charles De Gaul, there used to be a list of selected names. The parents had to choose the name from that list only. After De Gaul died, this list was destroyed and people were again free to choose their own names.

In 1853, no black could enter Illinois city without paying a fine of 50 dollars. He was allowed to stay only for 10 days. If he stayed further, there was another fine of 50 dollars. In case he was not able to pay this fine, he could be sold in the slave market. *(Asimov Book of Facts)*

Laughter is the best medicine. But in Helena, America, this medicine was banned after 7 p.m. No one was allowed to laugh after 7 p.m.

All the male barbers were out of job when in 1988, Iraq Government declared that no male barber could work in a hair cutting salloon. From time to time, it was checked out by a flying squad and anyone not carrying out the order was punished. *(Times of India)*

Make-up has always been associated with women. But in 1770, a bill was passed in British Parliament which banned the use of make-up. It said, any lady using make-up would be treated as a witch and would be punished.

Eating onion from 7 a.m. to 7 p.m. was banned in Waterloo, Nebraska for the barbers.

■■

Sale ... sale

A Volcano on sale? Yes, a volcano near Lenzoret in Canary islands was on sale. It was an inert volcano. The set up was that of a fairy tale. A small opening at the bottom of the volcano led to its inner core. There was a small beautiful house with a garden in front. This whole place was available for 1,95,000 dollars.

Or may be you wouldn't mind spending a few more dollars and go in for a well established, well equipped modern city near North Oregon. This well established city was built in 79 acres of land with 27 fully furnished bungalows, 20 other buildings, cinema halls, theatre, gymnasium, shops, restaurants, playgrounds etc. It may sound a better bargain to those who can easily spend 1.2 million dollars. Originally this city was established by American Airforce in 1951 as their Radar Base Station.

A submarine was on sale in 1987 at New York. The advertisement in New York Times described the capacity of the submarine as 70 persons and that it could be used both in and out of the water. No details about the seller and the price were given. *(Times of India)*

An atomic power house was built in Long Island, New York in 1984. For the next four years, the power house remained closed as the authorities found it unsafe for public. They said that it was too close to city. In 1988, this 5.3 billion dollars power house was sold to New York State for a mere 1 billion dollars. *(Times of India)*

Only 4000 dollars for a Centurian Tank? In 1989, Swiss government decided to replace its 30-year-old Centurian tanks with latest German Leopard II tanks. While some of these Centurian tanks were demolished, the remaining were put on sale. *(Times of India)*

World's biggest brothel 'the daily planet', fully airconditioned with 16 lavishly furnished rooms and an indoor swimming pool, is on sale. The buyer will not regret his decision as the place promises a good return.

World's tallest building 'Sears Tower' in Chicago, Illions, USA was on sale in 1988. This building is 1454 ft. high and has 110 floors.

(Guinness Book)

Islands are very much in demand. Now and then, one gets to hear of their sale and purchase. One such island was Giga island near Western coast of Scotland. Its area is around 3400 acres and the expected cost is around 3 to 10 million pounds. *(Times of India)*

The costliest song of the world is 'Happy Birthday to you...' The copyrights of this song are reserved with Wirchatry Ltd of New Jersy. The owners of this company is Sangstank family. They had taken the copy-rights for this song in 1935. Since then, they have taken many companies to the court for unauthorised use of this song. In 1988, Wirchatry Ltd. decided to bring out the cassettes of this song. They expect to have a sale of approximately 12 million dollars till 2010. Since the duration of copyright in America is 75 years, after 2010, this song will become public property. *(Rajasthan Patrika)*

■■

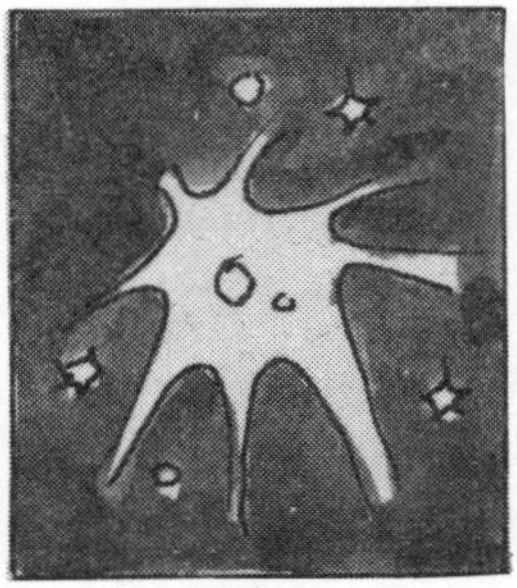

Disappearance !

Frizeland was a small island in the South of Greenland. The island is said to have trade relations with Greenland and other European countries between 1550 to 1560. It is an amazing thing that this huge piece of land just disappeared from the face of earth. The old maps of that time still show Frizeland whereas modern maps do not have it.

The 'Liberty Bell' was a beautiful piece of art. It was 7 ft. long and weighed 13,000 pounds. It was put on public display in 1893 at Interna-

tional Columbia Exhibition. After the exhibition, the bell could not be found anywhere. It just seemed to have disappeared into thin air.

Not only islands, even the continents have been found to have disappeared. It is a mystery as to how the Atlantic Continent which was very much there in ancient times, is nowhere to be seen. According to Pluto, this continent was there around 3200 years back. It was well developed and was very rich in natural resources. It is said to have been destroyed in a volcanic eruption.

There is another island which disappeared after 26 years of its discovery. In 1962, a Spanish ship came across this island between East and West Falkland. In 1988, when another ship tried to locate it, the island was nowwhere to be found.

A huge lake disappeared in seconds. This lake was in Italy. It was there from times immemorial. Children would play around. People went fishing in the lake. One day while everybody around the lake were busy among themselves, an amazing incident occurred.A huge whirlpool started from the middle of the lake and within five minutes all the water

disappeared leaving the lake high and dry. There has been no explanation for this sudden disappearance of the lake.

Now it was the turn of arms to get lost in the middle of the sea. 60,000 guns which were on their way to Britain from India, just disappeared in 1987. Any clue about these guns is yet to be found.*(Nav Bharat Times)*

Heavy water is used in Atomic power stations. In 1983, 15 ton heavy water was sold by Narsk Hydro to a German firm in Frankfurt. The whole consignment just disappeared on the way. *(Times of India)*

Where there is a will...

John Cameroon Young always had a secret desire. He wanted to know how a piano sounds when it is dropped from a helicopter. However, his wish remained unfulfilled. When he dies, he left 15000 dollars to his friends, out of his 8 lakh dollars' property. His good friends, who were aware of John's secret dream, got together and decided to fulfil it. They arranged for a helicopter and a piano and threw it down from a height. The piano landed with a loud bang. The friends left home satisfied that John must have heard the noise from up above. *(Times of India)*

Like every dog every pig has its day. In 1990, a pig in Dewonport became a millionaire when its master Margo Lamp left all his money (6 million dollars) to the pig.

Dorothy Walker was an 80-year-old widow. She left all her money to 'Royal Society for the Prevention of Cruelty to Animals' of London. This millionaire did not leave a single penny to her sister who was not so well off. *(Times of India)*

People, all over the world, are always asking God for something or the other. But Ernest Figweed Portmouth was an exception. He lived a simple life and before he died, he left all his savings 26,107 pounds to Jesus Christ. *(Times of India)*

It was a drunkard's paradise. Mr. Parkins was a rich British businessman who was very fond of drinking. In his will, he wrote that on his death all the doors of his house should be kept open. Anyone passing by should be called in and offered free drinks.

Do not blow money in smoke but smoke for blowing money. Ismail Brant left a will saying that his wife could only inherit his property if she smoked 5 cigarettes per day. Mrs. Brant hated smoking.

People make strange wills. Seventy-six-year-old Ernest Kelly of Hampshire left all his money to USSR. Kelly lived all his life in London and never once visited USSR. To his dear brother, Kelly left some old rusted gardening equipment. *(Times of India)*

You may inherit Madam A. Clara Gunjman's wealth if you could be the first one to reach Mars. This money is still lying with French government, waiting for its rightful owner.

Pand Smoe wrote in his will, "All my life, my wife took me to be a fool, which I am not. That is why I am leaving just one dollar to her. My son gets only enjoyment which he always indulged in and which is about the only thing he is capable of doing. My servants get my clothes which they always wore behind my back. My drivers get my old cars which instead of running just rattle under their able supervision. Finally I leave all my property and money to my beloved maid who always remained in background meekly without ever asking for anything."

Tale of authors

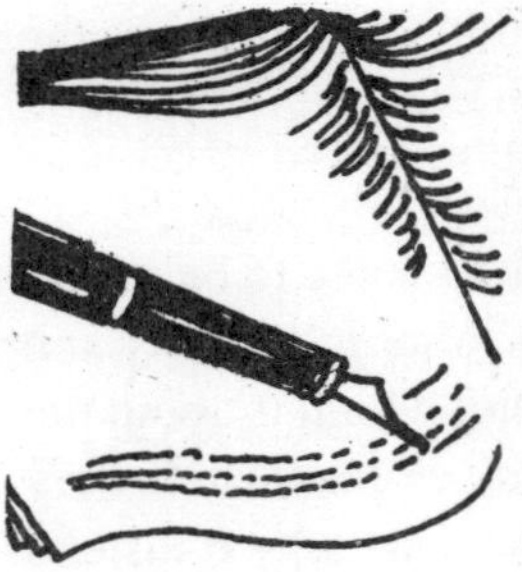

When Daniel Defoe wrote *Robinson Crusoe,* 250 years ago, no publisher agreed to publish the book. In all, 20 publishers refused to take chance on this new writer. Later, all of them regretted their decision when the book turned out to be a best seller.

Milton's *Paradise Lost* is a famous book today but when it was published, only 50 copies could be sold from the first edition.

William Shakespeare's name is a milestone in literary world. It is a pity that during his lifetime, the great writer could not get proper recognition. None of his plays could be published during his lifetime.

The author of the famous book *Crime and Punishment* had a bad habit — gambling. Many times, he had gone bankrupt. Most of his earnings went into paying for his debts. Ultimately when the debts kept on mounting, he ran away to Switzerland.

Several publishing houses took a chance on Clifford Irving and now want to forget it. Irving presold a ghost-written autobiography of billionaire Howard Hughes and got more than 1 million dollars in advance. The work was exposed as total fiction and Irving went to jail for 17 months. He had to pay back all the money he had received and went bankrupt in 1976 when he could not pay 7 lakh dollars to his lawyers as their fees.

He wrote his own obituary. America's famous writer, Will Rogers died in a plane crash in 1935. He had partially completed his last newspaper column before he began the fatal flight. The last word Rogers had typed was 'DEATH'.

Horashia Elgar wrote 119 books. All his books were for children in which he gave them the message of hard work and sincerity. He earned millions from the books. But the tragedy was that he died in severe poverty because he himself spent all his money lavishly.

There can be no comparison between 12 cents and 11000 dollars. But these are the different prices of the same book. Edgar Allan Pee sold his first book for 12 cents. Some time back the same book was resold for 11000 dollars.

A nurse who cared for a poor writer's child was paid with a manuscript. Rudyard Kipling told the nurse. 'This manuscript might be worth money some day.' Years later, she decided to take him at his work and sold *The Jungle Book* for money that allowed her to live in comfort for the rest of her life.

Professor Hideo Nishioka is the secretary of Japan Toilet Association. He has opened a museum in Minami Megome town near Osaka where bathroom sink-shaped-ash trays; urinal type flowerpot and 400 types of toilet papers are on display. He even wrote a book *Cultural History of Toilet Paper* which is quite popular. *(Times of India)*

Author Georges Simenon was like a writing machine. He was born in Belgium in 1903. He published his first novel at the age of 17 by writing it in 10 days. He used 16 different pen names. In all, Georges has published more than 150 novels under his own name and 350 under various pseudonyms. He was so fast that he finished one of these novels in exactly 25 hours.

■■

The ghost

'Awd (old) Nance' has been staying at Burton Agnes Hall at Yorkshire (England) for a long time. If someone tries to take it out of that Hall, the entire place starts shaking. Loud cries and sobs can be heard all over. With the result, each time Old Nance is put back at its favourite place. Old Nance is a 300-year old skull.

(Amazing Ghosts)

On 19 May 1536 Anne Boleyn was on her way to Blickling Hall in her horsecart when she was killed. Every year, the same day a horsecart can be seen travelling from the Tower of London to Blicling Hall. The eyewitnesses describe it as a frightening sight as the horse, the driver and Anne are all headless. *(Amazing Ghosts)*

Reef of heaven is situated in Federal State of Micronasia. The local residents believe that the place is cursed, due to which no one can spend the night in this place. 100 years ago a German Governor insisted that he did not believe such unreliable news and spent the night there. He was found dead the very next morning. The place is open for tourists during the day but is totally deserted at night. *(Times of India)*

A chess star Victory Corchnath claims that he has been playing with the ghost of Grandmaster Geeza Marouzki since 1984. Geeza died 34 years ago. His ghost plays with Victor through a medium Robert Rolland. the interesting thing is that Rolland himself does not know the ABC of chess. *(Kadambini)*

April fool

Sometimes people can experience imaginary things. On 31 March 1976 British Geologist, Patrick Moore, announced on BBC that tomorrow morning at 9:47, the planet Pluto would hide behind Jupiter. This would result into an upward pulling gravitational force. It may reduce our weight and we will feel lighter. Next day, on 1 April, many persons experienced it. Some even rang up BBC and told them with all sincerity that they have lost some weight.

But, not everyone can take a joke in good spirit. On 1 April 1989, a Sri Lankan newspaper *The Davasa* published a crossword puzzle and announced that whoever came with the answers before noon would get Rs. 10,000. The publishers found themselves in a soup when more than 200 persons turned up. When the publishers tried to tell them that this was only meant to be a first April joke, no one believed. Public refused to budge from the newspaper office without collecting their 10,0000 rupees.

People would believe anything — it only depends on who is telling them. An authentic source may even make them believe that spaghetti grows on trees. On 1 April 1957, a popular BBC announcer Richard Dimbley showed a film on TV in which spaghetti was shown growing on trees. People believed him.

First April, not always, is a day of fools. Reserve Bank of India started functioning from 1 April 1935.

It was a nosy affair. On 1 April, the headline of Dutch newspaper was that they were printing this edition with a special ink made of tulips. Thousands of readers rubbed their noses on the paper to smell the flowers. Alas! there was none. Then the realisation dawned upon them. They were made April fools. *(Amazing Hoaxes)*

Thousands of people rang up BBC giving their opinion about the bill. They were surprised to know when the telephone operator told them that they were made April fools. *(Amazing Hoaxes)*

On 1 April, a headline in Daily Mail was – "10,000 brassieres hinder the TV transmission". The news said that these brassieres were made of a special wire. The body heat and the nylon brassieres generated electricity which was conducted through this wire, thus hindering the TV transmission. Believing the news, a British Telecom officer issued a memo to all his female employees asking them to to wear such brassieres at work. *(The Hindu)*

■■

Paintings

Vincent Van Gogh's portraits are worth million dollars today, but the famous painter could sell only two paintings in his lifetime for a total of 84 dollars.

A modern art museum in New York displayed Henry Mache's painting 'La bet'. For 47 days, people came and appreciated the painter's work. An amazing fact came out when the painting was taken off — all these days the painting was hung upside down.

The painting of 'Mona-Lisa' is among the most famous in the world. When it appeared in the Metropolitan Museum in New York, each visitor was allowed only a ten second glimpse.

Some items have also been considered as fine art — a work called 'Room Temperature' with two dead flies in a bucket of water; a sculpture called 'Stone Field' made of 36 boulders and even some bricks which were kept at Tatty Art Gallery in London.

■■

Sex

Everything is fair in love and war — even a honeymoon in the Sahara desert. Michaell Asher and Mariantionietta decided to go to the Sahara desert for their honeymoon. The scorching sun, the parched lips, even the rumbling stomachs could not dampen their spirit. The two love bugs fully enjoyed their 271 days long honeymoon. *(Times of India)*

The Golden Fleece Condomary – a boutique in Holland sells only different types of condoms.

Fiedel Figura was a drug peddler. He had been suffering from stomach-ache for some time. Doctors decided to operate upon him. When they opened Fiedel's stomach, instead of carrying on with the operation they called the police. They had found 46 condoms full of drugs from Fiedel's stomach.

(Times of India)

Tit for tat. A young doctor in Tel Aviv met his match. The doctor went to a hotel and asked them to arrange a girl for the night. When the girl entered his room, both stood stunned. The girl was none other than his own wife. Next time this couple met only in court, for divorce.

■■

Sports

It was just not their day! In Munich Olympics 1972, the Basketball final match was being played between Russia and America. The Russians were winning by 49-48. Only 6 seconds were left when American player Collins got two free throws. Within seconds, the tables turned, and the score was now 50-49. Americans started jumping with joy at their unexpected victory. Just then a Bulgarian referee pointed out that there was still one second left before the game finished. The Americans played for one more second and went back to their celebration. Then came a British referee who declared that there were still 3 seconds left. Poor Americans had no choice but to go back to the field for the third time. It was in these three seconds that Alexander Belov, a Russian player, managed to score 51-50 and won the gold for his country.

In 1936, India was playing a cricket match against England. The English team was fielding. Alf Gower was the bowler. In his third ball Gower came running and instead of throwing the ball towards the batsman, he kept on running. He passed the umpire, pitch and the audience and went straight into the pavilion with the ball still clutched in his hand. Later, it was revealed that the poor baller had suddenly felt the urge to go to the toilet so badly that he had no time to even hand the ball over to anyone else.

Is it possible for anyone to win a silver medal without taking part in games? R.A. Christie was chosen for Indian Hockey Team which was to play in 1962 Asian Games at Jakarta. Later on, due to non-availability of foreign exchange, Christie could not accompany the team though his name was very much in the list of players. It so happened, the hockey team played without Christie and won silver medal. And Christie whose name was still in the list got the medal, sitting at home.

In 1936 Olympics at Berlin, everyone was expecting the previous year winner Stella Walls of Poland to retain the gold medal in 100 metre race. Much to their disappointment, at the last moment, Helen Stefens of America won the race. The angry Polish accused Helen of being a fraud. They accused her of being a man disguised as woman. To resolve the controversy, the judges decided to have her physically examined. Helen had to take all her clothes off in front of the lady officers in order to make them believe that she was a woman. Only after passing this test, she could be declared the winner.

A special cricket ball for blinds was made in South Africa. The ball was fitted with small bells whose ringing indicated the direction of the ball. This ball can still be seen in Lord's Cricket Gallery.

Nature

According to the Chinese news Agency Shinhwa, in December 1987, the residents of Chigtao witnessed a rare sight at a tourist spot near Laoshan mountain. They saw two suns rising on the horizon. Both were of the same size and 10 m apart. They remained there for 1 minute, then one of them started losing its shine and gradually disappeared.

Seventy km. from Xingiang in China is situated a sand hill, which can talk. From time to time, different voices can be heard from there. Sounds like passing of train, aeroplane, motor can be heard if a person rubs his body against the sand.

'Wiacliaza' city is in Polland. No cement, bricks or limestone have been used in this city. All the houses, their roofs, walls, floor, roads, churches, hotels even the gardens are built by cutting salt rocks around the area.

French scientists have developed a new species of chicken. This chicken has six legs and four wings and is equal to 3 chickens in size. This new species has proved to be a boon in hotel business.

A lamb was born outside Jamia Mosque at Nairobi in 1988, with 'Allah' and 'Mohammad' inscribed on its body. While standing, 'Mohammad' could be read on its back and whenever it would lie on its back 'Allah' could be seen.

A calf was born in Washneijh which had 6 legs. This calf was so active that at the time of birth it did not let its mother clean its body, immediately it got up and ran away. The calf weighed 24 kg. at the time of birth and after 8 months its weight increased to 240 kg.

S trange bird with black head, white neck and a red patch in the middle of its neck is on display at Royal Scottish Museum since 1 April 1975. The bird is called the Bare Fronted Hoodwink. It is an imaginary bird made by Willie Sterling.

Every year BBC plays some trick or the other and people get trapped each time. On 1 April 1977, Tom Jacksow, the Chief Secretary of British Union of Post Office Workers announced on BBC that the government has passed a bill accepting the German system of mailing addresses. Very soon, Britishers will be required to write the name of the lanes before the house numbers. Tom appealed to everyone to oppose the bill strongly.